GW00374712

FROM BELFAST TO HONG KONG

Brendan McCann

Published by

MELROSE BOOKS

An Imprint of Melrose Press Limited
St Thomas Place, Ely
Cambridgeshire
CB7 4GG, UK
www.melrosebooks.com

FIRST EDITION

Copyright © Brendan McCann 2011

The Author asserts his moral right to
be identified as the author of this work

Cover designed by Jeremy Kay

ISBN 978 1 907732 12 6

All rights reserved. No part of this publication may be reproduced, stored in a
retrieval system, or transmitted, in any form or by any means electronic, mechanical,
photocopying, recording or otherwise, without the prior permission of the publishers.

This book is sold subject to the condition that it shall not, by way of trade or otherwise,
be lent, re-sold, hired out or otherwise circulated without the publisher's prior consent
in any form of binding or cover other than that in which it
is published and without a similar condition including this
condition being imposed on the subsequent purchaser.

Printed and bound in Great Britain by:
CLE Digital Solutions. St Ives. Cambridgeshire

FSC
Mixed Sources
Product group from well-managed
forests and other controlled sources

Cert no. TT-COC-003115
www.fsc.org
© 1996 Forest Stewardship Council

Dedication

Dedicated to my three late brothers:
Billy, Pat and Gerry.

Gratitude

My sincere thanks to my wife Ann:
My most patient and stalwart supporter.

Photograph

By April Rooney:
Enniskillen, Co. Fermanagh, N. Ireland.

PART 1
THE EARLY YEARS

CHAPTER 1

MY EARLIEST MEMORY WAS BEING UPSIDE DOWN in some sort of cart. I was to learn later that it was my pram that was being manoeuvred by my older brother Séamus. The reason for this strange behaviour was to save his embarrassment, as a group of school kids who were known to him were approaching our location. Séamus didn't want to be seen pushing a pram, which was taboo on the streets of Belfast, even at the tender age of nine and a half! On that particular day Séamus didn't mind walking me and had tried to persuade me to come out of the pram, with a view to hiding the offending item behind some bushes nearby. Even at my age of about two and a half I was prone to bribery, and as my older brother had nothing to offer for my co-operation, I saw no reason whatsoever to conform. Thus the reason for my unusual circus act! If my mother ever discovered how many different activities my pram was used for, with me in or out of it, I'm uncertain how long Séamus, Tony and Maura would have lived (*more about Tony and Maura later*).

It sometimes amazes my siblings the extent of my memory programme, a talent that I was to depend on in future years more often than not.

My birth was an unusual occurrence; not the fact that I was born and not knitted *(of which I was accused in later years)* nor being the youngest of ten, but the way upon which I entered this world. I am reliably informed that my mother gave birth to me at home; again, not that unusual but becoming less frequent in the backstreets of Belfast. The only other person at home on 15th December 1953 was another of my brothers, Billy. Billy was about sixteen and a half and enjoying his usual fry-up at about six o'clock that night, when my mother called out that the baby was on the way! The midwife was due to visit to arrange transportation to the local hospital, but apparently I had other ideas. Billy alone tended to our mother, who gave birth to her tenth child, a sturdy and most handsome son, one of eight sons and two daughters. The midwife arrived shortly afterwards, and to Billy's relief took control of the situation. Billy returned to his fry-up and finished it before it got cold! After considerable consideration my mother put three possible names on a small sheet of paper, Brian, Brendan and Michael. She then very carefully picked up a pin, closed her eyes and stuck the pin into the paper. After hitting none of the names on at least three attempts, the pin finally hit the name of Brendan! The baby days that followed did not register in my memory bank due to the fact I was very young at the time!

By the time I was born, in 3 Ballymurphy Road, the two eldest of the family, Frank and Robert, had already left or were in the process of leaving home to join the Irish Army *(more about Frank and Robert later)*.

My eldest sister, Monica, was to leave soon after. I was told in later years that on one of her return visits she discovered I hadn't been baptised (christened).She promptly took me to the local church and had the necessary done and also became my godmother! Monica's other cry to fame was that on another visit she saw me running around the house wearing only a vest *(for any smart Alecs, I was about two and a bit at the time)*. She bought me my first pair of underpants.

The circus act with Séamus and the pram took place somewhere near the next address after Ballymurphy Road. The reason for our move from a three-bedroomed house with bathroom, garden, hot and cold running water, to a tenement two-roomed flat is unclear. Possibly the fact that the rent, amongst other things, wasn't paid was a vital part of the local council's decision to move us to 64 Clifton Park Avenue. The words Park Avenue sound great even to this day but, alas, not only did the seven remaining children of the original ten still live at home but Mammy and Daddy had to share the two rooms with us.

The two rooms were living and sleeping accommodation with a small coal fire in the bigger of the two, and a small gas light on the wall of both. We shared the kitchen and toilet with another tenant. There was no bathroom, but what I remember most was the long steep flight of stairs leading from the front hall up to the first floor where we lived. I had many near mishaps going up and down and quite often had raw legs from sliding down the banister! The biggest problem I had was the carriage of water. From what I can remember, although we lived on the first floor, the kitchen with the drinking water was on the ground floor. One of my daily tasks was to make sure the big bucket for the drinking water was kept full throughout the day. Not so bad on the way down the long steep staircase, but the return journey was a monumental feat to say the least! The bucket when three quarters full became not only heavy but awkward. This led to spillages on the stairs, the first floor landing and on my clothes. Young as I was *(about four and a half)*, I was determined to think of a plan to ease my burden. I decided not to carry the big bucket but to use one of Mammy's small cooking pots and make several journeys in order to fill the big bucket.

After countless journeys up and down, up and down, up and bloody down, I swore for the first time in my life. *Fuck this!* If that crowd wanted drinking water, they could get it themselves! My new lease of independence did not last long. Mammy made sure of that.

One of the few memories I have of my Father *(he died when I was about nine*) was going with him to the snug in the local pub where I first heard the phrase '*A half and a half*'. I still use the same phrase to this day and take great delight explaining its meaning to bar staff in various locations on my travels. A half is a half pint of beer; the second half is a large whiskey. In Northern Ireland in those days, the spirits were sold in quarter gill measures so a large whiskey was a half gill measure, thus '*A half and a half*'.

On the British mainland, spirit measures were sold in fifth or sixth of gills, resulting in the average Belfast man consuming alarming amounts of whiskey etc. throughout that country, particularly in the London area where most of my family moved in later years.

If I was a good boy and didn't tell Mammy how many drinks Daddy had drunk, I was given a fizzy orange and a packet of Tayto cheese and onion! A treat that featured in my early talent competition days with Séamus and Tony a short time later.

It was on the way back from such an excursion that I had a slight mishap. Daddy was holding my hand as we crossed a patch of waste ground, when I decided to chase some birds that were feeding off a few scraps of bread. It had been snowing earlier that day and the ground in general had become very slippery. Needless to say, I went arse over tit and landed on what appeared to be a broken milk bottle! My left wrist was cut open from left to right with a piece of glass protruding from the injured area. Daddy nearly had a fit! To this day I'm unsure if it was the possible seriousness of the cut wrist, or Mammy's reaction to the situation that worried Daddy the most! Anyway the cavalry arrived in the shape of my brother Pat who was about fifteen at the time. He told Mammy what happened, then he and she rushed me to the Mater Hospital for treatment. The route to the hospital took us past the Crumlin Road Jail, a place Mammy had said was '*where all the bad boys go, with the man in the big tower watchin' over ye'*. This was my first taste of being treated like a celebrity. It wasn't until years later that I realised how serious the injury could have been. Future trips with Daddy were few and far between and one of my brothers had to be present. My brothers were queuing up to go with us. This meant that Daddy had not only to buy me a drink, but also buy one for the minder. None of my older brothers would settle for a fizzy orange!

Even in those early years there was always music about the house. Saturday nights around the fire, beer and lemonade etc. on the table, Maura singing, Gerry singing, Pat, Tony and Séamus playing guitars and singing, spoons playing, me banging pots and pans, and some-times a treat of fish and chips. Billy was rarely asked to sing a song. Billy was without doubt the world's original shite singer! We used to give him a comb and a piece of paper so that he could make a noise! It's funny how the fun nights are always easy to remember, and the not so fun nights are pushed to the back of my mind.

On another memorable occasion, I was playing in an overgrown garden of a derelict house, which had a dodgy old wall stretching along the front. This acted as a playground for my pals and me for our daily war games or cowboys and Indians. After going through the actions of being wounded (*none of us ever got killed, no matter how bad our imaginary injuries were*), I fell off the dodgy wall, helped by some of the loose bricks, and fell in a heap into the jaggy nettles. The stings of the jaggy nettles on my arms and legs had me jumping up and down like a jack-in-the-box! Whether it was the fall, the bricks, or the swift reaction to the jaggy nettles I'm not sure, but I developed an almost unbearable pain in my left shoulder. Being blond and a wee bit daft, I climbed up back onto the dodgy wall again! I thought to myself, '*How do I explain this one to Mammy?*' While I sat there feeling sorry for myself, not realising that I could find myself in the same situation if I sat there much longer, the cavalry arrived in the shape of my brother Gerry, who was about sixteen and a half at the time. Gerry was coming home from work, and if he saw me in the street he would normally pick me up and carry me on his shoulders. When he tried to lift me off the wall I let out an almighty cry of pain. He immediately realised this was more than the usual whinge for attention. He got me home pretty fast, and I had to do some pretty fast thinking to explain why I had been playing in a place where Mammy had told me *(in no uncertain terms)* not to play! Mammy had a fair bit of knowledge about basic illness, breaks etc., and Gerry agreed it could be serious. So once again I was rushed to the Mater Hospital for treatment. Once again the route took us past the Crumlin Road Jail, where Mammy said that I would end up if I didn't stop being a bad boy! The good news was I had a broken collar bone and had to wear a sling; once again I had a taste of being a minor celebrity.

When I was about five we moved back to Ballymurphy Road (*it was just before I started primary school*). We moved into number 32. Another three bedrooms, bathroom, a small front garden, and what appeared to me to be a huge back garden that was to become an adventure playground for Tony, Séamus, Maura and me. On the days of good weather we would put on a concert in the back garden. The backyard was at ground level; however, there were steps leading up to the large back garden which acted as our stage. Not only did we perform music but also makeshift circus feats. During one such feat Tony and Séamus instructed me to put a cardboard box on my head and stand halfway along the garden. They then tossed a coin to see who was going to take the first shot with the longbow and arrow! This weapon was for real. Where those two got their hands on a longbow and arrow in the back streets of Belfast is beyond comprehension. If I wanted to have a turn with this weapon that was used by real live Indians, I would have to show that I was a brave member of our wee gang.

Anyway, I did what I was told, and Tony won the toss so he got first shot. A few seconds later I was lying on the ground screaming blue bloody murder. Thankfully the arrow fell considerably short of its target area and hit me just below my left knee. Again I was lucky that the tip of the arrow was a wee bit blunt and fell out of the wound when I hit the ground. Maura appeared and stood in absolute disbelief; not the fact that we had created this ridiculous situation, but the fact that it was a crap shot! Tony promised me the world if I didn't tell Mammy. With help from Séamus and Maura he cleaned my wound, and I settled for a gigantic 99 ice-cream from Mr Whippy! No sooner had I eaten it when I ran into the house as Mammy came home from the shops, and through big Bambi tears told her the whole heartbreaking story of what had happened to the baby of the family! Needless to say, there was a great deal of blood, sweat and tears that followed. Mammy said, *"If it's not his bloody father trippin' him up, the wee fella himself trying to be a kamikaze, then it's the rest of the eejits in the house tryin' to kill him."* I was cuddled for days afterwards.

Not long after that particular escapade Christmas was on its way. I was always going on about getting a three-wheeled bike, and being the devious little bastard that I was, I was laying it on a bit thick, especially after the incident with the longbow and arrow!

Mammy was saying how expensive a new bike would cost and that I may have to wait until the following year. However, the cavalry arrived, once again in the shape of my brother Pat. Now, Pat was working as a waiter in the Grand Central Hotel, in Royal Avenue in Belfast. Coming up to Christmas, I believe, was very good for over-time and tips. My face was an absolute picture when, one night after work, he walked through the door with a brand new three-wheeled bike! I will remember to the day I die the excitement, the joy, the whoops from everyone else in the house when this *magnificent* bike was revealed! It was one of many favours he was to deliver, up until the day he died, many years later.

At the earliest opportunity I was out and about riding *my* new bike; but like all good things, they need to be shared, so that's when Tony, Séamus, Maura and I formed our one-vehicle, four-man display team! We were fantastic, and as it was *my fuckin' bike*, I got to decide who was next to be the driver, who would be balancing on the back, and who would sit on the front handlebars. Once again I was a minor celebrity!

CHAPTER 2

A T THE RIPE OLD AGE OF FIVE and a bit I started school at St Kevin's on the Falls Road. It was all boys, which I thought was great. My first teacher was Miss Moss and she was very nice.

I don't honestly remember her ever raising her voice in my first two years at school, although I have to say she would have had good reason on many occasions, not with me of course. Most of the kids would fight over anything. Fight over the free milk, fight over the free dinners, fight over who was first in the toilets, fight over the green and black snotters! At least once a week, some wee fucker would shite himself just to get out of school early. The sight of the shite running down his legs was like a mini tidal wave, especially as he was wearing short trousers that hadn't been washed since before they ended up in the rag store! If it was done in this day and age it would probably get an award as modern art in motion.

My headmaster was called Mr Mount who, like Miss Moss, was a most likeable character; however, nothing on earth could have prepared me for what lay in store in the guise of my primary three teacher, Mr Rodgers. He was a tall man in his late thirties with dark wavy hair. How in God's name he managed to live to that age without being assassinated is beyond belief. He was a Jekyll and Hyde, psychopathic, sadistic bully, who could smack you around the head from ten yards and you wouldn't see his hand go back into his pocket! If by chance you were

9

out of range, the wooden blackboard duster would be launched like an Exocet missile, with absolute pinpoint accuracy. This man was, without doubt, a professional bastard! I was overjoyed to learn that I would be attending another school due to the fact we were moving house again.

Sometime between moving houses, Tony, Séamus and I formed a wee trio of song and dance, in preparation for a Saturday morning talent competition at the Forum Cinema in Ardoyne. Tony played guitar, Séamus had a set of soup spoons to supply the rhythm, and I was the star of the show because not only did I sing better than the other two eejits, but I realised that I could sing, swivel my hips, wiggle my legs, and use a hula hoop all at the same time *(wearing my best short trousers)*, to the astonishment of the audience and the judges! We only bloody won the competition and were presented with a crisp new ten-bob note. So, off we went to the shops to decide how much of our winnings we would spend, and how much we should give to Mammy. I was made to wait outside while Tony and Séamus went into one of the shops to buy some goodies. When they came out with a brown bag containing the goodies, they ran round the corner to an old derelict house, whereupon the contents of the bag were revealed. I got a fizzy orange and a packet of Tayto cheese and onion! *Fuck me, not again!* Tony and Séamus produced bottles of beer and a few loose *fegs,* with smiles like cats who had got the cream. In order to keep me from telling Mammy about them drinking and smoking, they let me try a few sups of beer and a few puffs of one of the fegs.

I promised myself then, as I would promise myself many times in the future, *never again!* We could have been Belfast's answer to the Beegees. We could have been the McCanngees! Unfortunately, due to circumstances beyond my control, fame and fortune would have to wait for now.

We moved to an area near the centre of town called the Pound Loney, or just the Loney. It was an area of small terraced houses, in long narrow streets, encompassed within three main streets, Albert Street, Cullingtree Road and Divis Street, and overshadowed by the tall regal towers of St Peter's Cathedral (*in those days it was known as a Pro cathedral*). No one could give me a satisfactory explanation of how the area got its name. Once again I could not understand why we left behind a nice big house with gardens, and settled for a two-up and two-down with no bathroom, no hot running water, and an outside toilet. Maybe it had something to do with the rent, *again!* Our new address was 12 Scotch Street and, believe it or not, once we sorted ourselves out I came to love the street, and all its unusual and sometimes strange customs and characters.

By this time Billy had moved to London and was earning very good money although, while the average Belfast man in London was earning big money, he was also spending big money. Most were paid on Friday and broke on Monday!

Gerry, who had a great education at St Malachy's School, a nice office job, and had found his forte in life as a lead singer in quite a few different bands, was also being chased by screaming women, and decided to move to London to better himself! HOLY FUCK! Was the man deranged?

Pat had also flown the nest. He joined the British Army, in a regiment called the Irish Guards, more affectionately known as the 'MICKS'. Little did I realise how much of an influence Pat's decision would have in relation to my future choice of career.

Sometime throughout this period Tony was back and forward to London. Quite often, on his visits home he would stay with us or at his girlfriend's house over in Millfield.

So, in our wee house in 12 Scotch Street there lived Mammy, Séamus, Maura and me. Daddy was around, I'm just not sure where. I believe he was probably drinking and wouldn't come home, thus sleeping it off somewhere else, or more often than not he was in hospital, due to the lifestyle that was, and often remains, synonymous with many Belfast men. The whole of our street knew every man, woman and child, cat, dog and canary who lived in the street, such was the close-knit community that could be described as claustrophobic, but in which I thrived. Handball, pitch 'n' toss, marlies, rallyo and hango, were just a few of the games we played, hail, rain or shine.

At seven and a half, after a long period of religious study, I was to make my first Holy Communion. This was indeed a proud day for Mammy and me. The only problem was, before the big day I would have to attend my first official confession! How in God's name was I going to remember all the sins I had committed, and what was the parish priest going to say when he found out what I had been up to! I was worrying myself to death, and even thought of becoming a *Protestant!*

Then it came to me like a flash from hell; I mean, heaven. Don't tell the parish priest everything; just juggle the numbers a wee bit. Speak to the main man himself in heaven above, deal with the organ grinder, not the monkey, and all will turn out for the best. My first confession and first Holy Communion went better than I could have prayed for, and what a surprise I got when I counted all the money I was given to celebrate the great day. I knew then there's money in this here religion.

By this stage Frank and Robert had each completed a five-year period in the Irish Army, married Dublin girls, Frank to Maura, Robert to Anne, and had begun to settle down to married life. Frank and Robert were both, as were their wives, devout Catholics, champion ballroom dancers, and non-smoking teetotallers! Frank and his family moved to London and then to Cambridgeshire where they live to this day. Robert and his family spent a short period in Birmingham and then returned to Dublin where they also live to this day. On many occasions I would spend part of my school holidays with Robert and Anne in Dublin. Not many kids in Belfast, much less the Loney, got much more than a day trip to the local seaside, and here was me going all the way to Dublin!

Neighbours in Scotch Street had relatives in Dublin who would often come to Belfast to visit. One of their sons, who was about my age, became a regular playmate and his mother had said that I should visit them on my next trip to Dublin. The son's name was Danny and he was always called Danny Boy. Now, Danny Boy was a bit of a chancer. He quite often boasted about how easy it was to make extra pocket money for very little work, carrying bags, suitcases etc. at Amein Street Railway Station (now Connolly Station).

I thought that maybe I would try it out when I next went to Dublin. It wasn't long before our paths crossed again, and my first attempt at becoming an entrepreneur was to prove most enlightening.

After a few brief encounters, Danny Boy and I had agreed to meet one morning while we were both off school for the summer holidays. When I arrived at the station Danny Boy laid down the plan for the day. It was really very simple. To avoid any unnecessary competition, rivalry, or confrontation between us, we would simply share whatever payment we got 50–50. As Danny Boy said, "*Roight,*

13

you give me half of what you get, and Oi'll gives you half of what oyez get, roight?" I thought that maybe I should keep my wits about me, just in case he tried to diddle me.

We both waited patiently for the first big train to arrive. The smaller trains were from local areas bringing people to work, and very few would be carrying heavy bags or suitcases, and would have even less to give you a decent tip for your trouble.

All of a sudden we heard this deafening hissing and screeching sound. It was the Belfast train coming in. We began to move along the platform, together at first, and then we split up, like a military manoeuvre, and then I saw *him*: this huge rotund man getting out of the first-class compartment. He was certainly a man of the cloth, dressed in a huge crimson cassock, with an equally huge crucifix hanging from his equally huge neck, and the jewellery worn on his hands would have made the Queen in London green with envy! He seemed to be looking over the tops of the heads of the people passing by, possibly expecting someone to meet him. Before Danny Boy could get into his stride, I sprinted along the platform and skidded to a halt. When I looked at him up close, he looked like a Christmas tree on legs!

"Carry your bags, sir?" says I. He grunted his approval and pointed into the carriage, in the direction of two huge suitcases. Was there nothing about this man that wasn't huge?

I dragged the suitcases, one at a time, from the train, being careful not to scratch or damage them. No sooner had I done that and he was off, with me struggling along behind, carrying a suitcase in each hand, and *him* glancing over his shoulder every so often telling me to keep up, and Danny Boy nowhere to be seen! When I reached the top of the stairs at the exit, the walking Christmas tree was standing at the bottom, talking to a man wearing a peaked cap next to a big fancy car. Both men waved me down the long flight of steps, which

I descended most carefully. When I finally reached the boot of the car, the driver had to practically prise my hands from each case. Due to the heavy load I was carrying, when I rested the luggage on the ground, my hands had locked around the handle of each case! When the driver eventually secured the luggage into the boot of the car, he held the door open so that the big fella could squeeze himself into the back seat. Just before he got into the car, the big fella put his hand into his pocket, hopefully to bring out my tip.

A few minutes after they left, Danny Boy showed up looking for his half of the tip. For those who aren't familiar with a blessing, it is performed with the right hand starting above the head, going downwards to the waist, then left to right in line with the shoulders. Danny Boy said, "*Roight, gimme half of what ya gat.*"

I gave him the first half of the blessing, from head to waist.

About ten minutes later a garda on a bicycle arrived outside the station, where I was educating Danny Boy in the art of teamwork. The garda asked, "*Have you seen the little Belfast boy who swore at the Bishop?*"

I replied in my best Dublin accent, "*Ah now, Sur. Sure he went home about foive minutes ago.*" Needless to say, my partnership with Danny Boy dissolved soon after, although we stayed in touch on and off for the next few years.

At the age of about eight and a half, I was admitted into the Royal Victoria Hospital to have my tonsils and adenoids removed. Apart from the normal mumps, measles, breaks and sprains, this was the first time I would have to stay in hospital overnight. It was also the first time that I got a bed all to meself! I was there for about four days and what an experience it was. All my meals were served to me in bed, the nurses were all fussing over me, Mammy brought me lots of orange and lemonade and fruit and sweets.

I thought to myself, hey, I really do enjoy being a minor celebrity! Anybody can rough it.

Back to school after those summer holidays was the beginning of another series of adventures. My new school was called *St Brendan's!* Imagine going to a school with the same name as me and, believe it or not, I was the only Brendan in the whole school! Once again I felt like a minor celebrity. It was a mixed school and I made new friends pretty quickly (*not with any girls*!).

The layout of the school was a wee bit strange to say the least. The classrooms were spread out around the local area. There were two classes in a large hall, which also served as our dinner hall, about five minutes away from the main building; another class in another building about five minutes away in the opposite direction; and the remainder of the classes were in the main building of the school. The ground floor of the school had a large room on the right which held two different classes, primary six and primary ten. The remainder squeezed into individual but very cramped rooms. Although I was in primary five in the large hall some distance away, I was soon to move into primary six, in the same room as primary ten. There was a nice big fire in the centre of the facing wall, with space enough to walk down between the two inside rows of desks of each class.

My first day in the dual classroom proved to be most entertaining. First of all, let me explain why the classes went all the way up to primary ten. There was simply no secondary school close enough to send those aged 11+ to be educated in. If anyone was ever clever enough to qualify for grammar school, the cost of school uniform, transportation and additional school activities would be beyond the reach of any household budget; consequently they operated under the old outdated system of providing classes 8, 9 and 10. So there I was, being taught by Mr Tracey, and a few feet away Mr Christian was not teaching, but attempting to maintain interest and discipline in a class of what appeared to be couldn't-give-a-fuck wasters!

Very few of the senior class had little to look forward to except the dole queue, more commonly referred to in Belfast as the Bru. The system had let them down very badly, and of course most of these young fellas had become rebellious, uncooperative, and almost out of control, but Mr Christian had the measure of the class on most occasions. Although the school was mixed, there were no girls in the senior classes as there was Secondary Education in a local school for girls called St Louise's, more affectionately known as the Brown Bombers because of the awful brown uniform they had to wear.

Anyway, whoever made the decision to collocate 6 and 10, whose curriculum was completely different, must have had a degree in arseholes! Plus the fact that we in primary six were given examples of how not to behave by the seniors in primary ten! The continual banter from across the room was at times absolutely hilarious, and I nearly pished meself on quite a few occasions on that fateful first day. I began to realise after a very short period of time that they weren't all wasters; they were just trying to make the best of a difficult situation that was no fault of their own. The one-liners and wisecracks that were flying around the room on an almost daily basis probably founded the base upon which my sense of humour developed in later life. This was to become an absolute tribute through my teens, adulthood and through to middle age; may it never die. Those fellas in primary ten sure taught me 'don't let life get you down!'

CHAPTER 3

F OLLOWING ANOTHER PERIOD IN THE ROYAL VICTORIA Hospital, Daddy died in the early part of 1963, when I was nine and a bit. The days that followed his death were a bit hazy to say the least. I'm not sure if all the family turned up, I'm not sure if all the family wanted to turn up, but the turnout for the funeral was very large. His body was laid out in his coffin at a local funeral parlour. The usual custom was to have the body laid out in the family home, as was the way with every other funeral in our street. Maybe there was more room in the funeral parlour for the many grieving friends and relatives who wanted to pay their personal condolences; I don't really know. Tony took me to see Daddy. I was very apprehensive at first. I had seen several corpses before at other houses in our street, but when it's your own Daddy it's hard to drum up the same blasé attitude, especially when there are only two of you in a small, dark, eerie room. Tony said, "*Just say a wee prayer.*" We both stood there for a few minutes, not really knowing if the other was praying for Daddy, looking at the dark red velvet curtains that seemed to cover every inch of the walls, and the hint of me feeling sorry for myself because that's what I thought I should do. When Tony decided that it was time to leave, we both had a wee tear in our eyes.

On the day of the funeral, the requiem mass was celebrated at St Peter's Cathedral, and I remember people I didn't know coming up to Mammy and me to offer their condolences.

Then, through the crowd, a hand came out and gave me a pat on the shoulder. I looked up and to my utmost astonishment, saw that it was my headmaster, Mr O'Neill! As our eyes met, he said, "*You'll be okay, Brendan.*" I didn't cry any more that day.

In 1960 Pat, as I said before, had joined the Irish Guards. At first we didn't see a lot of him, due to him going to England for his basic training, and then after a period of leave he was posted to Germany. From there he was posted to Chelsea Barracks in London, therefore he was able to come home more frequently.

It was not long after Daddy's funeral that I remember a crowd of guys calling into the house every so often. They came from all over Belfast, all over Northern Ireland, some from as far away as Dublin and Cork, and there was this fella with a funny accent, from Liverpool! The Scouser's name was Steve Griffiths. Steve and his wife and son (*who was a few years younger than me*) called in for a cup of tea on their way to one of Steve's relations, who lived some-where out in the country. Steve was to relate this occasion to me when we met again many years later. Little did I know that the visits from these guys would be the beginning of a series of parties, sing-songs, card games, joke-telling sessions, and just generally actin' the eejit! I was being sucked into the world of the Micks!

Because we lived quite close to the City Centre, our wee house in the Loney became a meeting place for loads of Irish Guards coming home on leave, returning from leave, going out for a night on the town, or just somewhere to crash when they couldn't get home. Very often when I came downstairs in the morning, I would have to step over sleeping bodies all over the small sitting room and kitchen floors! On more than one occasion somebody had fallen asleep in the outside toilet; with his trousers still sitting around his ankles! But the *craic* was ninety! The most frequent visitors were a group of Micks from in and around Belfast: the Montgomery brothers, the Sullivan brothers, Vic Buckley, Davey Maxwell, Jacky Sinclair, Noel Stevenson, Brian Blair and Jimmy Wynn, to name a few. Although Mammy didn't drink very much, the Micks would take it in turns to buy her a small bottle of Harvey's Bristol Cream sherry, or coax her to go around the corner to the pub *(the snug, of course),* and have the *craic* with her before the Micks went into town. Mammy loved the banter they all had together, and if the truth be known, she treated them all as if they were her own sons. One fond memory I have of Davey Maxwell was when he arrived back to our house in the wee small hours, slightly worse for wear. Not wanting to go to his own house in Dee Street for fear of upsetting his parents, he arrived outside 12 Scotch Street in a taxi, stumbled out, and proceeded to serenade Mammy so that she would let him in! He also had a wee drop of sherry with him. In later years when I would want to get the better of him, I would say, *"Uncle Maxy, remember the time when you serenaded my Mammy?"*

He would say, *"Come on now, young McCann, the least said about that the better!"*

These strange Micks were great fun to be with. No sooner had they returned from leave when another one would rap on the door, just to say hello on their way home on special leave, for whatever reason. Tall men with tall tales, or wee men with even taller tales! They certainly brightened my day up. As soon as I saw one of them walking up the street I knew the *craic* was going to be great!

In and around all these visitors, there was always something going on in the street; as I said before, everybody always knew everybody else's business. If there was a hint of scandal, tongues would wag, exaggerations would amplify a situation out of all proportion, and when the whole saga became out of control, the effing and blinding would start. God Almighty, these people could swear and cut you to the bone, especially the women! Some of the most memorable phrases were;

1. Get yer *bastards* off the street.
2. Yer only a *hoormaster*.
3. Sure yer ma's da was a *fuckin' black and tan*.
4. Yer ma sucks *dicks*.
5. Yer head's a *fuckin' marley.*
6. I *rid* yer wee sister, and yer big sister's a *sponkbox*.
7. I'm not one te talk behind any body's back *but...* she pays *the tic man* in many different ways.
8. Jesus, Mary and Joseph, don't have me *fuckin' swearin'.*
9. Away and wash yer *fuckin' oxturs.*
10. Yer da's a *fuckin' bollixs.*
11. Hey, wee girl, do ya *buck?*
12. Show us yer *diddies.*

Absolute stars, every one of them!

There was a stocky wee man who lived two doors down from us, in number 8. He was known to everyone in the street as Mad Rabby. If any of the kids as much as walked past his door, he would go buck mad! Sometimes when he would leave the house, he would carry a grubby old pillow-case, with a quantity of unknown items inside it. My mates and I were most curious as to what he might be carrying, because it looked quite bulky at times. Could it be rolls of banknotes, or gold or silver nuggets, or could it be *dynamite?* One day we decided to follow him.

He was always dressed in an old dark grey suit, wearing an off-white T-shirt, a pair of light brown shoes that were scuffed at the toes, with almost no heels at all; we don't think he wore any socks. Oh yes, he was completely *bald!* Anyway, Joe Watson and I were the only two of our group of mates who had the gumption to follow him; so off we went, keeping a discreet distance behind him, sometimes walking on the opposite side of the road, sometimes splitting up and keeping in contact with hand signals. Most of the time he walked so fast Joe and I were almost running to keep up. Maybe it was a *bomb* he had in the pillow-case, and he needed to get it to someplace before it blew up! I thought *'If it goes off, we could be on TV*!' Eventually, we arrived at a house in Boundary Street, which was just over the other side of Divis Street. Mad Rabby had a quick look over his shoulder, and went inside without knocking the door, a sure sign he was up to no good. We waited for what we thought was ages, and nearly went home, when out of the house he came with what appeared to be an empty pillow-case folded under his arm. A few seconds later a woman came out and shouted, "*Rabby, come back on Friday afternoon, not Friday morn, and I'll have all yer washin' ready for ye.*" With that, Joe and I burst out laughing, and returned to Scotch Street with a very tall tale for our mates that would have put even the MICKS to shame.

A few days later Mad Rabby wasn't too well and the doctor had to make a house call. Next thing I know, the doctor is at our front door looking for Mammy. He had an unusual request for her. I couldn't believe my *fuckin' ears!* The doctor explained to Mammy that Rabby needed several prescriptions, and due to the fact that Rabby didn't like going into a chemist's shop, would Mammy allow *me* to go and get them for him. Mammy agreed straight away and the doctor said, *"Send him down to Rabby's anytime this afternoon. He shouldn't be too long."*

Me going to Mad Rabby's on my own, it was a fuckin' suicide mission! I was convinced he had spotted Joe and me following him a few days earlier, but there was no way out for me, the cavalry were definitely *not* going to arrive this time. So, later that afternoon, dragging my heels, I reluctantly made my way to Mad Rabby's house. I had told no one of my mission that was to be my downfall, least of all my mates. I rapped the door very, very, lightly. All of a sudden, Mad Rabby opened the door and dragged me in! I began to panic as I looked round his wee sitting room; there was no proper wallpaper on the walls, they were covered from top to bottom with neat squared-off sheets of *newspaper*, and the place was absolutely spotless! *"Oh my God, I am very sorry for having offended thee"* (start of an *Act of Contrition*).

"What are you muttering about, wee lad?' says Rabby. *'Here's the prescription the doctor gave me, and here's two bob(10p) fer yerself, for being such a good boy. Now don't be too long, and if you get the message right you can go to the shops for me when I need somethin' else. It's not every day you can get a wee lad from round here you can trust!"*

Off I went to carry out the task in hand, and I said to myself, *'There really is a God.'*

Another unusual character who could be very entertaining was an oul fella called Jimmy. Now, Jimmy was middle-aged, going bald with a Bobby Charlton wave, tall, well-built and lived with his aged mother in either number 17 or 19.

At least once a week, sometimes twice if he had a few extra bob, he would get blind drunk! He would end up in the middle of the street, usually late in the afternoon, wearing his socks with a matching hole in each heel, minging old corduroy trousers and a string vest that carried enough bacteria to cause an epidemic of biblical proportions! In his right hand was a half-bottle of brandy or whiskey, and his left hand appeared to be conducting an imaginary choir, or even an orchestra! Jimmy didn't sing like normal people, he sort of chanted out of tune with the rest of the world; and he always chanted the same old phrase.

"Up the *aye are ray*, up the *aye are ray*, the Peelers are fuckin' bastards, up the *aye are ray*."

Sometimes when a few of us were feeling a wee bit brave, we would get pretty close to him and mockingly join in: "Up the *aye are ray*, up the *aye are ray*." We would join in the dance that was more of a stagger, waving our hands in the air: "Up the *aye are ray*." When Jimmy finally realised what was going on he would attempt to lunge at us each in turn, and scaring the lives out of every one of us!

On one particular day, we could hear Jimmy ranting and raving inside his house and his wee Mammy pleading with him not to go into the street to *"make a holy show of yerself!"* A few minutes later out he came; a sight that was to be emblazoned on my memory forever! Jimmy staggered into the street to perform his usual cabaret act; this time he definitely surpassed himself. He was wearing his usual socks and string vest; however, there was nothing in between except his huge willy john (my Mammy's pet name for such things). His balls looked big enough to carry in a wheelbarrow, and there was enough pubic hair to make a dozen coconut mats! Then the *piece de resistance:* he turned round and there it was – a great big streak of shite, stretching from the hairy cheeks of his arse, down the back of each leg and joining up with each sock; and then, as if in perfect tune, he chanted, "Up the *aye are ray*, up the *aye are ray."* Nobody could stand up straight or even talk: the sight before them was absolutely hysterical! Jimmy's Mammy came out and screamed at him like a banshee; his answer to her was "up the *aye are ray."* Eventually Mammy ran over to give Jimmy's Mammy a hand, and they got him back indoors. However, Jimmy did leave a few wee *Maltesers* behind in the street.

Sometime throughout all this mayhem, Billy and Tony were home from London, and popping in and out of Scotch Street. Billy had married a girl from Cookstown called Tish, and by this time they had three children. Initially they lived in London, returned to Belfast for a while and then back to London. Where Billy's family was living at the time of this next entertaining episode, I'm not too sure.

One afternoon Mammy was busy in the kitchen as usual, Tony had gone out that morning to see some old mates, Billy was studying the form in the paper in the wee front sitting room, Séamus was sitting on the front doorstep, Maura was out somewhere *again*, and I was reading a comic next to Billy (as if I too was studying the form). Séamus was about sixteen at the time and was quite tall for his age, so Billy decided to use Séamus as a runner to place his bets on at the local bookies, which was at the junction of Cullingtree Road and Albert Street, less than two minutes' walk from the house. The bet was quite complicated but Billy had written everything down, making the job in hand for Séamus and the man in the bookies easy to carry out.

Now, previously to this when we lived in 32 Ballymurphy Road, our family and another family, known as the Smiths, had a disagreement over the lending, borrowing, damaging or whatever it was, of a single or possibly two guitars *(I know it confuses me still, to this day)*.

Anyway, the Mammy of the Smiths came to our house in Ballymurphy Road to complain and seek recompense. I remember our Mammy answering the front door to this very angry and frightening woman, with me peeking through the window in the hall to get a good look at what was going on. The woman began to get louder and louder, then all of a sudden Mammy grabbed Mammy Smith by the throat, and gave her a fantastic 4D one *(Belfast slang for a* good right hook!). I thought to myself, *fuck me, it's the clash of the Mammies*. At this point Mammy Smith fell backwards over our wee fence, arse over tit, landed in our front garden with her dress up over her shoulders and exposing the finest pair of bright red passion killers any woman of substance could ever wish for!

Now, some years later one of the Smiths, namely Ted, was visiting some friends down in the Loney and was standing outside the very bookies that Billy had sent Séamus to on that fateful day. Ted was about twenty years of age, and while talking away to his mates, of which there was about four or five *(when Séamus told this story, it was about twenty-four or twenty-five),* Ted recognised Séamus as the son of that McCann woman who had beaten up his Mammy a few years before. Although Séamus was quite tall for his age, he was no match for an even taller and more experienced Ted Smith, especially with four or five other hard cases looking on. Ted stood at the only door of the bookies, blocking the only way in, and to make matters worse he stood on Séamus' toes, preventing him from getting someone else to place the bet. As soon as the race started Ted stood back, laughed, pushed Séamus in the chest to the whoops and laughter of the others, who were encouraging the intimidation of this lone McCann.

When Séamus managed to get back to the house to tell Billy of his plight, Billy was not pleased to say the least. All three of us settled down to watch the first race; Billy's first horse got chinned! Every cloud's got a silver lining because all of Billy's horses would have to win for him to win his accumulator, which would have been a pretty penny had they all come in, but that was beside the point. A wrong-doing had to be put right! Meanwhile, Ted Smith and his cronies had gathered across the street from our house, with smirks on their faces, pointing at our house, and every so often howling with laughter. Billy observed them for a while, considered sorting a few of them out; however, if he did so he would be guilty of the same crime of intimidation that Ted Smith was guilty of. Billy decided to wait until Tony arrived home later that day, and allowed those across the street to have their fun, *for now!* Lo and behold, Tony arrived home and was duly informed of what had gone down earlier that afternoon.

Billy explained his rationale, Tony agreed, and what was to follow was to be talked about by many a man in the Loney for many a day.

Tony looked through the window and made sure of his target, then out through the front door and across the street. At this stage Ted Smith with his gang of cronies *(that had grown to about six or seven in number)* saw Tony swiftly approaching and decided to square up. *Big fuckin' mistake!* Within only a matter of a few seconds, Ted Smith was lying on the deck with a face like a monkey's arse, two of his cronies had sore faces for attempting to intervene, and the remainder were backing off as Billy got closer. I shouted to Mammy, *"Mammy, Mammy, come and see, there's a big fight in the street and our Tony's winnin' it!"* The next thing I know, Mammy's at the front door screaming at Tony to get into the house saying, *"Sure ye shouldn't be fightin in the middle of the street, what the hell will the neighbours think?"* Thus endeth the lesson.

A short time later Pat arrived home on leave. The first morning he came off the Heysham boat was the normal bedlam of countless Micks appearing for the much sought after *Ma McCann's breakfast!* Now Pat was very proud of the fact that although he had a variety of smart casual outfits with him on leave, he had also brought with him two very smart new suits. Both suits were three-piece, one charcoal grey, the other and his favourite, navy-blue. Depending on the occasion, Pat would sometimes elect to wear the grey suit during the day but would always keep the blue suit *(his favourite)* for night time, especially if he was meeting up with a wee honey. On one particular occasion Pat had been down town drinking with a load of Micks, in their favourite watering hole in Ann Street, the Capstan Bar. Pat met a wee honey and after a wee coort, he arranged to meet her that night in town and take her to one of the local dancehalls in York Street called the Orpheus.

On Pat's arrival in the Loney he had a quick pint in the Gaelic Bar, which was on the corner of Bow Street and Cullingtree Road, telling the locals how lucky he had been that day with this wee honey, and how he would sweep her off her feet that night when he met her wearing *his favourite* three-piece navy-blue suit! Off he went round the corner to Scotch Street into the house, which at this stage was empty except for Mammy and ME. Pat was whistling and Mammy said, *"Jesus, son, you must have had a good day out with yer mates. Come and sit down and have a wee bite to eat. You'll need something in yer belly before ye go out drinkin' again, won't ye?"*

Pat replied, *"A sure, Mammy, I met this wee honey today and she's meetin' me tonight down the town to go dancin', so she is. After I have somethin' te eat, I'll have a top 'n'tail and get into me flash suit and I'll be out late, or stay in one me mates' houses, so don't you be worryin."*

Anyway, Pat had a big plate of mince stew and off he went upstairs to strip off, put on a couple of towels and came downstairs; had a shite, shave and shampoo and then skipped up the stairs to put on the smellies over his bits, put on his clean underwear and *EEEmaculately* pressed shirt; then, to his horror, *his favourite three-piece navy-blue suit* had vanished from the wardrobe!

Attached to the hook of the vacant hanger was a white pawn ticket! On the back of the ticket was a very short scribbled note saying, *'Yer suit's in the pawn, Pat, thanks for the drink. Billy!'*

Needless to say, the air turned blue! While Mammy was trying to calm Pat down, the cavalry arrived in the shape of my goodself.

"Pat," says I, *"sure you've got yer nice grey suit up the stairs, sure the wee honey hasn't seen ye in that yet. Give it a wee press and you'll luck just as good, won't ye?"* Pat's answer to that alternative was a great big smile, and two bob (10p) for me. I never ever did find out the outcome of that navy-blue suit but I'm sure the both of them are having a laugh about it now, up in heaven.

CHAPTER 4

THE NEXT MEMORABLE EVENT IN MY LIFE was my first trip to London! By this time Monica had married Ted, a docker from the East End of London, had their first child, and were living in the capital city in an area called Peckham. I was about ten at the time and prior to the trip with Mammy, all my mates and I were surmising what it would be like to travel all that way and actually stay there. They all made me promise that I would send them a postcard each!

The afternoon of our departure was filled with hand-waving and cheers, some from the neighbours but mostly from my mates. It was a warm and pleasant evening and I was ready for the first of quite a few journeys on the Heysham boat, and to put the icing on the cake, a taxi picked us up to take us to the docks! Once again, I was a minor celebrity.

The dockside was packed with passengers waiting to board the boat, but before long we were on board in a queue at the purser's office. Mammy was hoping that a berth (cabin) would be available for our overnight sailing. In those days it worked out cheaper to pay for a berth on board than to book one in advance at the same time as your ticket. It didn't take long for Mammy to use her Belfast charm: *"I'm only a wee woman on me own, with me wee boy who's frightened to death of crowds."* Ten minutes later we were in our wee cabin with bunk beds and a wee sink; it was a fantastic experience and Mammy said I could have the top bed. I was up and down those wooden ladders about a dozen times when Mammy said that we would go out for a wee dander. I couldn't believe the amount of people that were on the boat; I don't think health and safety laws these days would allow such overcrowding. After a wander round the few shops, we decided to eat our pre-prepared sandwiches and crisps in the cafe. Mammy paid for a cup of tea for herself and a glass of Coke for me *(I had given up the fizzy orange for the time being).* Once again I could not believe the amount of people that were squeezed onto the boat, and Mammy said that they were still allowing more passengers to board. The boat was soon under way and we made our way back to our wee cabin. I told Mammy that I needed to go to the toilet. We weren't sure where the Gents were so I told Mammy that if I couldn't find them I would ask a member of the crew *(seizing my chance to explore, on my own).* I was up and down, round and round, got lost at least twice and then got lost again; strayed into the bar area, and by this time I really did need to go to the toilet, so off I went into the Gents situated in the bar foyer.

I took two steps into the toilet, went at least three feet into the air and landed hard on my elbows and arse! I looked round me and realised not only had I slipped on the wet floor but was now lying in a sea of pish and vomit. Depending on which way the boat was rolling would dictate in which direction the smelly substance would creep, from one side of the floor to the other. Then there was a shudder as if the boat had hit a large wave and the inevitable happened. The overflowing urinals splurted upwards, and I was drenched in small droplets and particles to the extent that I, too, added to the decor and contributed to the mass of wall-to-wall puke etc. that was increasing by the second! I wanted to scream for Mammy but what explanation could I possibly give for being there in the first place! Finally I managed to get to my feet, and made my way through the door to the bar foyer. A wee woman took one look at me and immediately said, *"Come with me into the Ladies and we'll get ye cleaned up, son."* Once again the cavalry arrived and saved my bacon! By the time I found my way back to our cabin, Mammy was dozing slightly. She stirred just a wee bit and I said, *"I was only away for ten minutes,'* to which she replied, *'Ock sure, yer a good boy for yer Mammy!"*

The remainder of the journey to Heysham was uneventful but it was great snuggling down in me own wee bed, in our own wee cabin, with our own wee sink. I also learned a short cut if I needed a PISH through the night that I was to use for many years to come and more so as I got older. *Think about it!*

The next morning we were woken by a steward who kindly provided us with tea and biscuits. Mammy said that she felt like Royalty and I thought to myself, *"What would the gang in our wee street say, if they could see me now?"*

Once again I felt like a minor celebrity. A short time later we washed and dressed, made our way to the area of departure, waited patiently for the gangway to be lowered and eventually made our way from the boat to the waiting London train. I made sure I got a seat next to the window and before long Mammy got some toast for herself, sausage rolls for me, all washed down with a cup of tea each. Although I really enjoyed the scenery and the wandering up and down the train, the excitement of the journey caught up with me: I dozed on and off for most of the journey until Mammy gave me a shove and said, *"We'll be there in about ten minutes, son."*

Although it was around 1.00 p.m. when Mammy woke me, my first impression of the big city was how grey, dark and bleak it looked. *"Are ye sure this is London, Mammy?"* says I. *"I bloody well hope so,"* says she. *"We've been on this train for bloody ages, and if this is not London, that conductor man will know all about it!"*

At that precise moment in time the conductor stopped at our seats, and informed us that this was in fact the last stop, London Kings Cross. Off the train we went, along the platform to be met by Monica's husband Ted. I thought to myself '*Fuck me, look at the size of him! If he gives me a belt round the ear, he'll fuckin' **kill me!** I'd better behave meself!*'

We all made our way by car across London to Monica and Ted's flat in Peckham, with me not knowing which way to look and for how long, just in case I missed something of interest. I related my head movement to that of a horror movie I saw many years later, *The Exorcist!* The following two weeks were spent being looked after by Monica and Ted, visiting friends, relatives and quite a bit of sightseeing. However, there were two instances that remain in my mind's eye to this very day.

Ted took me to the pictures (cinema) to watch *Gunfight at the OK Corral*. At home everyone was talking about this new movie that was coming to Belfast, starring Burt Lancaster and Kirk Douglas. It was being advertised throughout Belfast as the best western *ever made!* In those days a major movie such as this, although well-advertised well in advance, would take forever to reach the screen in Belfast cinemas and here was me being taken to see it in London! *Fuckin' great!* Anyway, Ted and I walked the short distance from the flat to the local cinema. On arriving, Ted asked if I would like some chocolate to which I answered yes, most enthusiastically! So off Ted went, and got the tickets and chocolate while I had a nose around the foyer. The overall layout of the cinema was much the same as those back home but much more of a flashy finish. When Ted returned with the tickets, he handed me this *ginormous* bar of Cadburys chocolate *(they didn't sell them that big in Belfast!)* that put a huge smile of delight on my face and also gave me peace of mind that he wasn't all that frightening after all. After my obligatory well-mannered thank you, we went inside to take our seats. The music began, the movie came to life on the screen, and I began the dismantling of *the big bar of chocolate*. It took me two 'sittings' to eat all of the chocolate and I soon became aware that something was missing, a cold drink! Now, being a well-mannered wee soul, I didn't want to be seen to be 'kickin' the arse out of it' by being cheeky and asking for a cold drink on top of the tickets and the big bar of chocolate, so I decided to go to the toilet and get a drink of water while I was there. After washing my hands with hot water that scalded the fuckin' life out of me, I let the cold water tap run for a while to get a nice cold drink.

On and on it ran and it ran, and it fuckin' *ran.* It bloody ran a fuckin' *marathon!* Still no cold water, it wasn't even luke-fuckin'-basterdin' *warm!* In the end, I was so thirsty I took a gulp of water anyway! *Agggraaa!* I nearly puked, but I needed to wash away some of the chocolate, part of which was lodged at the back of my teeth, and another piece had wedged itself to the roof of my mouth with the warm water making matters worse! I returned to my seat beside Ted, who enquired, *"Allwite, san?"* I just nodded and said nothing. Soon I was feeling nauseous and uncomfortable; my attention to what was going on in the movie was becoming non-existent. I thought to myself *'What's Ted goin' te say if I keep runnin' in 'n' out te the toilet?'*

A wee while later I made an excuse, and almost sprinted back to the toilet, unfortunately to no avail. I decided to go to the front of the cinema to see if a bit of fresh air would help with my problem, and would you believe it; the cavalry showed up, in the guise of a lovely wee woman who had paid for some sweets and a paper cup full of Coca-Cola. She asked if I was all right. I explained that the heat inside the cinema was a lot greater than what I was used to back home in Belfast, so she kindly offered me a drink of her Coke.

Nearly breaking her arm, I accepted her kind offer, drinking almost half of it, thanking her, and then disappearing back into the auditorium in a matter of a milli-second so as not to miss too much of the movie! When I arrived back at my seat Ted said, *"Allwite, san?"* To which I replied, *'I am now!'*

Throughout my time in London my brother Gerry was on leave from the Merchant Navy, and he introduced Mammy and me to his girlfriend Jo McGuire, who was later to become his wife. Even at my young and tender age I realised that Jo was a hell of a looker! She came from a large family who were originally from Co. Mayo in the west of Ireland, and she was also very well-spoken. Needless to say she spoilt me rotten, not just on that trip but on many other occasions in the future. Anyway, Gerry and Jo had arranged to take Mammy and me to see a show in the West End! They didn't tell us where we were going so as not to spoil the surprise that was in store for us. Eventually we arrived at our destination, and what a surprise it was, to say the least! We were only standing outside the London Palladium!

I could hardly believe it! One of our favourite shows on television at home in Belfast on a Sunday night was *Sunday Night at the London Palladium*, and here's *me* walking through the front door as if I owned the place! *Fuckin' great!* Sweets and cold drinks were the order of the day and of course a big fancy programme to prove that I was actually there.

We took our seats which were about ten rows from the stage. I noticed in the join of the two seats in front of us were a small pair of theatre binoculars. For the princely sum of sixpence (2p) the binos could be released from their holder and used by any individual wishing to do so. Gerry obliged with the sixpence and there I was checking everyone and everything out. *'The gang are never goin' te believe me when I get home!'* This was so fuckin' *great!*

The show began with a dance routine by the Tiller Girls! There were about twenty of them with feathers in their hair, wearing minute sparkled body tops that covered from just above the tit line to just below the minge line and every one of them had gorgeous legs all the way up to their fuckin' necks! There were high kicks that almost reached the ceiling, and when they turned their backs to us the tight fitting costumes were so far up their arses, it reminded me of my Uncle Mick with his false teeth out *(more about Uncle Mick later)*. And what was I doing? I had the binos glued to my eyeballs and when Gerry asked to have a go, I told him to go and get his own!

The whole show was fantastic, with singing from one of the top cabaret stars none other than Frankie Vaughan and great comedy from one of my all-time favourites, none other than Tommy Cooper, unfortunately both of whom are now a long time dead. It certainly was an experience of a lifetime and for once the cavalry didn't need to arrive! Gerry really knew how to lay on a great night out; he was renowned for it until the day he died. He's probably up there now, organising that *great big party in the sky*, arguing the toss with Billy and Pat. Now, dear oul Mammy, wouldn't you like that?

When we returned to Belfast I held court for many a day with stories *(sometimes enhanced a wee bit)* of my exploits, adventures and what it was like being treated like a minor celebrity!

CHAPTER 5

Now, UNCLE MICK SULLIVAN MADE A GREAT impression on me when I was a wee boy. He was no blood relation whatsoever, but would sometimes call in to the house, especially when he was a bit flush. I first remember him coming into my life on the odd occasion when we lived in 32 Ballymurphy Road, but more so when we moved into the Loney. Uncle Mick lived in the Star of the Sea hostel for men which was located in Divis Street; thus the reason for his more frequent visits when we moved into Scotch Street. I found out many years later about his life in the Merchant Navy and his relationship with my maternal grandmother, whom I never met, known as Granny Kennedy.

Mick Sullivan was originally from Dublin and ran away to sea at the ripe old age of fourteen. After a period of working on local merchant vessels he progressed further afield and eventually served on very large merchant ships. He was involved in many hazardous journeys during the First and Second World Wars! He was torpedoed twice and was awarded a row of medals for his part on many life-threatening operations *(I sold the medals to a shop in Smithfield Market called Joe Cavanagh's)!*

A lot of his free time was spent in Belfast in an area known as Sailor Town. It was while he was on leave, possibly between the two World Wars, that he met and had an intimate relationship with Granny Kennedy. I have no idea where Grandad Kennedy was at this time, and I'm not too sure if anyone else knew of his whereabouts, but Granny Kennedy and Uncle Mick shared a house down near the docks. I also believe that the house was large enough for my mother, her siblings and some occasional lodgers, which was the probable guise that suited both Granny Kennedy and Uncle Mick. Anyway, he was always calling in to see us, and always had a pocket full of change for me and any other kids that were playing in the street. He frequently helped Mammy out with a few bob.

Although by this time in my life Uncle Mick was certainly in his seventies, he was still being contracted to work on ships that were in dry-dock in Belfast. He would normally work nights, possibly in the engine room, for a series of continuous shifts, sometimes for up to fifteen or sixteen hours at a time! Even at his age, in the Sixties he was earning the princely sum of £7 per shift, a vast amount in those days. Needless to say, he worked hard and played even harder. On many occasions he would be in the Gaelic Bar. Sometimes he would take me with him, and I would be allowed to sit in the snug and he would buy me... yes, you've guessed it, a fizzy orange and a packet of Tayto cheese and onion! If he decided to go walkabout and take me with him, frequenting many different pubs, my intake of fizzy orange and Tayto crisps was phenomenal. I remember Mammy saying on several occasions, *"How in God's name does that child get his underpants into such a state?"* In hindsight, my underpants could have been compared to Brands Hatch! I had many more days out with Uncle Mick and sometimes wonder if I got my nomadic instinct from him, as I too love to go for a wander when I go out for a drink, although my taste for fizzy orange and Tayto crisps has dwindled along the way, and I have someone else to wash my underpants now.

About eighteen months after Daddy died, Mammy remarried a lovely wee man called Paddy Kelly. Paddy was a widower with four grown-up children of his own (two boys and two girls) who all lived in either England or Scotland, and had (wait for it) a three-bedroomed house, with bathroom and running hot water, and front and back gardens! The address was 32 Northwick Drive in Ardoyne. The house looked great but I was very wary about leaving all my great friends and the street that I loved behind. Mammy reassured me that all was not as it seemed. I don't know how she did it but she managed to keep the house on in Scotch Street in the name of McCann, and the house in Northwick Drive in the name of Kelly, so I could visit my friends in Scotch Street whenever I wanted and, when possible, stay the night. My older brothers and sisters who were living away from home could also make use of it when they returned from their travels.

St Brendan's School was closing down, with the junior classes being moved to another primary school called St Comgall's on Divis Street, and the seniors to a new secondary school off the White Rock Road called St Peter's. My new address in Ardoyne qualified me for a place at St Gabriel's Secondary School where Tony and Séamus had attended when we lived in Clifton Park Avenue. Mammy thought if I didn't get into St Malachy's Grammar School, St Gabriel's would be the best option. So after a brief period at the Holy Cross Primary School I began my four year period at St Gabriel's. When Mammy and I were filling in the form regarding what my first and second preferences were to be for secondary education, first choice was St Malachy's, second choice was St Gabriel's. Now, if the truth be known, the paperwork was carefully adjusted to read St Gabriel's on both preferences! The reason for this was quite simply down to numbers: at St Malachy's you got an average of six homeworks a night with a binful at the weekend; at St Gabriel's you got an average of three homeworks a night and about four at the weekend. I remembered the time of my first Holy Communion; juggle the numbers a wee bit!

When I was asked at Holy Cross Primary School about the unusual choice, I explained that my two older brothers attended the same school and my Mammy thought it would make perfect sense for me to go there as well. Because I was only going to be at Holy Cross School for a very short period of time, and none of the staff really knew me that well, my devious plan was a success, and so it came to pass I attended St Gabriel's. I don't honestly know to this day if I passed the 11-plus or not!

Secondary school began early in 1965. Séamus, who was almost eighteen, was to travel to England to take up a job opportunity in Birmingham; Maura, who was about sixteen and a half, was working as a shop assistant.

The first day was full of new friends, some nice and some not so nice teachers, and an absolute binful of school books of different shapes and sizes. I was told that the schoolbooks would increase each day to coincide with all the new subjects we were to undertake, and all the books had to be covered in some sort of protective paper binding on the night they were issued, and shown to our respective teachers the following day! I thought child labour finished years ago! Anyway, the cavalry arrived in the shape of my sister Maura.

Maura's proper name is Mary Magdalen; we think Mammy was going through a holy phase at the time Maura was born but changed her mind after Maura was baptised. It was too late to do anything about it so Mary Magdalen has been called Maura for as long as I can remember. Imagine what it must be like to be called after the only whore named in the Bible!

Anyway, Maura was a professional book-coverer. I had the best covered books in the class. If the truth be known, even though she was a girl *(and still is)* she assisted me on many occasions to learn some of the most basic things in life: for example, how to read the clock, how to tie my shoelaces, how to say big words correctly, like hospital instead of *hosipal* and ambulance instead of *amulance*. I still can't say *filim* correctly. She had developed a great love for singing and encouraged me a great deal when I was to take up singing, drumming and dramatic art in the coming years. The only trouble with Maura was the hand-me-downs; can you imagine me going to school in a mini-skirt! Oh yes, she dragged me to see such great *filims* starring Cliff Richard or Elvis Presley and I had to sit in the middle of a load of screaming girls! What a fuckin' racket! It's tough being the baby of the family, but all Maura's friends treated me like a minor celebrity.

During my early days at St Gabriel's, I met my form teacher, Pat Brannigan.

Pat Brannigan influenced me more than any other teacher I had ever met, and I was delighted to find out that he would be my form teacher throughout my four years of secondary education, as long as I remained in the A-class, for example 1A, 2A, 3A, and finally 4A.

He was the most approachable man anyone could ever meet, whether it was personal, social, or schoolwork. He taught our class English, Drama, and Religious Knowledge. He was by no means a holy Joe, but shared Religious Knowledge instruction with other teachers at our school. He opened up a whole new world for me by introducing me to the delights of dramatic art and the Debating Society. I owe him much more than he could ever imagine!

School friendships began to foster, and the crowd I hung around with all tended to have the same interests: having great fun *(we were prone to practical jokes),* amateur dramatics on stage, arguing a point of order or a point of information at a debate and, last but not least, performing with the school choir. Although most of our class got on well, there were four of us who hung around together most of the time: myself, Brendan Baxter, Peter McAleese and his slightly older brother Brian. There was less than a year between Peter and Brian's birthdays, hence they ended up in the same class at St Gabriel's. The McAleese brothers lived in Ligoniel, Brendan Baxter in Silverstream, and of course I was now spending more time in Ardoyne.

Peter and I were also into sport such as soccer, Gaelic, hurling, swimming, and although we were not particularly tall, we played a bit of basketball.

We were a bunch of misfits who were channelled away from the normal unsavoury world of the sectarian divide by the personal dedication of one man, Pat Brannigan. *God bless him!*

Sometime later that year, when Tony was on one of his visits from London, he paved the way for me to join St Mary's Pipe Band situated in Divis Street. I had always been keen to take up drumming, but with all the activity at secondary school, I just couldn't get round to making the commitment; until Mammy had decided enough was enough!

I was always banging spoons or knives and forks on different things around the house, until one day when I was home on my own, I turned up the volume of the record player *full blast!* The cutlery I would normally use wasn't making as much noise as the music, so I decided to use the two pokers that were beside the fire. And what should I use as a drum? None other than the new tiled hearth of the fireplace! When it came to the jazzy drum solo on the record, I closed my eyes and really *let rip!* By the time the music had finished, the hearth was in fuckin' pieces! When Mammy found out, *I* was in fuckin' pieces!

Tony's girlfriend's father was the drum major of the said band; consequently, I found myself at the band practice very shortly after Mammy had finished having a *major* sense of humour failure!

It was the start of a very long, successful and most enjoyable hobby, kicked off with a brand new pair of drumsticks costing four and six *(22½p)* kindly paid for by Tony; he probably felt guilty over the money he and Séamus diddled me out of when we won the talent competition a few years earlier.

Not long after joining the band, Mammy decided we were on the move again, this time back to Scotch Street. The Council had realised that Mammy was not entitled to have *two* houses, and told her that she would have to choose one. Due to a major redevelopment scheme that was to take place in the Loney in the very near future, with all the houses knocked down, and a labyrinth of all-singing, all-dancing maisonettes, with one twenty-storey block of flats being built, with mod cons that would make your hair curl, Mammy chose the wee house in Scotch Street with a view of getting a brand spanking new place to live. So now there was Mammy, my stepfather Paddy and I living in Scotch Street, looking forward to seeing the new estate being built.

Maura had moved out and was living in a rented flat on the other side of town. Sometime during this period she met Séamus Doherty who was originally from Castlederg but was now working in Belfast as the head chef in the Midland Hotel; he was later to become her husband *(more about Séamus Doherty later)*. I remained at St Gabriel's School, which was my choice due to my new-found friends, and was able to carry on with my old friends from the Loney.

CHAPTER 6

L IFE IN GENERAL FOR ME, AT THIS point, was pretty good, what with lots of sport, drama class and the Debating Society *(both of which had progressed to additional night classes for those interested, of which I was one),* drumming *(a bit slow at first, because I was now doing it properly)* which was coming on in leaps and bounds, and discovering a novel way of making a bit of extra money without too much work involved.

Now, the normal way I made my own pocket money was helping the milkman or selling newspapers. The milk round was a very early morning start with wind and rain on most occasions; selling newspapers was an early evening start with the same amount of wind and rain! Carrying the huge bundle of newspapers from the city centre all the way up to the top end of the Falls Road, selling them along the way and making sure that the money was correct *(any deficiencies came out of your pay)* was no mean feat *(reminded me of carrying the water bucket, in Clifton Park Avenue).* Selling the newspapers gave me a much better chance of a tip, whereas the milk round, although easier on the feet, was limited to whatever the milkman decreed you would get paid, depending how little work *he* had to do. He was a lazy oul bastard!

Now, my mates from school, Brian, Peter and Brendan, had become altar boys at their local church. They had been recruited by their parish priest due to their predecessors leaving school for full-time employment. For whatever reason, that particular church was

43

very popular for weddings, and weddings means altar boys, and altar boys means money!

Normally, after the wedding ceremony takes place, the participating altar boys line up in an appropriately designated area *(with the senior altar boy on the right of the line)* to be thanked by the bride and groom. At this point the groom shakes hands with each altar boy in turn, and discreetly slips a coin into his hand. Usually half a crown for the senior altar boy **(12½p),** it decreases in value along the line until the last altar boy, who would get a sixpence **(2½p)** or a shilling **(5p)** depending on how generous the groom might be. On checking his hand, the senior altar boy would give a sly wink to let the remainder know that he had received a most acceptable reward.

Anyway, off I went to volunteer my services, having been highly recommended by Brian and the other two, and the parish priest was very pleased to accept this nice young fella into the ranks of his high-profile team of altar boys.

Because of my upbringing, my study and practice periods were relatively short, and I was soon asked to take part in my first wedding mass. Everything went according to plan; after the ceremony we lined up outside the church, near the beautiful flower beds, to await our just rewards. The bride and groom appeared, all smiles and luvvy-duvvy, and the groom approached the senior altar boy. They shook hands; the senior altar boy looked along the line at the remainder of us, and shook his head. I knew this was to mean that he had received nothing!

At this point I put my right hand under my lovely clean and pressed cassock, then inside my trousers, then inside my underpants, then round my balls; then I took it back out just in time to shake the tight-fisted bastard's hand! This unfortunate setback did not affect my commitment to the job in hand, and as sure as God loves a trier, I attended many future successful money-making weddings!

Although I was making a name for myself with the extracurricular activities at school, I was also beginning to show promise with the Pipe Band. My determination to get it right led to many days and nights of extra practice, which was making Mammy wonder if she had made the right decision by asking Tony to get me into the band in the first place. Anyway, one night at band practice I got my big chance to play on a real drum, and not just a practice pad as normal. After all the extra hours of practising rudiments and simple drum beatings, it was time to put the hard work to the test. What a disappointment. The feel of the drumsticks on a drum, with the drumhead made of tightened pig's skin, was much more difficult than I could have ever imagined. My sticks were bouncing all over the place and I found myself making a racket rather than a musical sound. *Fuck this for a game of cowboys!*

Just when I thought I had almost made it I was brought back down to earth with a bang; however, the leading drummer was very understanding and explained that this sort of thing happens to most learners at their first attempt. His name was Eamonn Dillon and his brother Séan was the pipe major. Now, Eamon wasn't the most natural drummer in the world *(he started late, as an adult),* but he could empathise with the learners, and offered a lot more encouragement than more talented players. He understood my plight and, determined as ever, I played on that oul drum until I was satisfied with my attempts to make some sort of musical progression, with Eamon in attendance long after everyone else had gone home. Within a few weeks, not only had I improved in leaps and bounds but I was now thought capable of playing one of the new screw-tension drums that had recently been bought, brand spanking new, for a lot of money which had left a large void in the band funds. Consequently I was warned to be very careful at this early stage of my tuition! Well, let me tell you, it was like a dream come true. They couldn't get me off

45

this brand new drum, it became addictive. I felt compelled from there onwards. I couldn't put my drumsticks down; as soon as I got in from school or had any free time, I was outside in the backyard practising on my drum pad. I would arrive early for band practice on Wednesday nights and Sunday afternoons and I would always be the last one to be kicked out at every practice so that Eamon or Séan could lock up!

Then came the day of my first band parade; there I was with my bonnet, jacket, kilt etc. It was the May Day Parade in Belfast, 1966. I wasn't the slightest bit nervous; I could hardly wait to get started, and then off we went, marching round the centre of Belfast. There were lots of people lining the streets, the sun was shining and I was having a great time, and Brian, Peter and Brendan from school turned up to watch me playing, as did quite a few neighbours from the Loney! About halfway round the route I began to feel slightly uneasy because my new brogues were irritating my heels. The pain didn't feel that bad initially but every so often we stopped, to allow the people and other bands in front of us to put a wee bit more distance between us and them.

That's when the pain and the realisation kicked in that to wear a new pair of brogues on such a long parade was not the wisest thing to do! Eventually the parade ended, we were given the order to dismiss, Séan and Eamon thanked us all for the excellent turnout and high standard of playing, Paddy the drum major expressed how proud he was to lead the band on our first May Day Parade; and I'm standing there wishing they would all *fuck up*, and let us go home as, by this stage, the pain in both my heels was like a throbbing pulse beat! Being too proud to admit that I was in agony I smiled at everyone, said my goodbyes and made my way by the quickest route possible and headed for home. Once I was out of sight I slowed down to what can only be described as a snail's pace, and walked in a fashion which would be reminiscent of that of an old man, or possibly likened to the drunken stagger of Jimmy, our neighbour in Scotch Street *(what goes around, comes around!)*. Due to the fact that I was a proper parading member of the band I was allowed, for the first time, to take my shiny new drum home with me! The unaccustomed extra weight and the slightly cumbersome load did me no favours whatsoever. The short distance home felt like miles of an uphill struggle, but pride and determination kept me going until, at last, I reached home and Mammy's welcoming arms. As soon as she saw me, Mammy got my brogues off, gently and slowly bathed my heels in warm water and administered first aid using antiseptic gauze lint bought from the local chemist. The sweat was *fuckin' drippin'* off me but the whole unfortunate experience stood me in good stead for the future.

Now that I had the drum home with me, it wasn't long before there was a small gathering in the hall of our wee house to view, touch and even try a gentle tap with a drumstick on this lovely, shiny, marooned-coloured drum. On one occasion there were that many mates who wanted a turn on the drum, I had to bring them into our wee sitting room, and before long there was that much noise Mammy was beginning to get a headache. She became very annoyed and said, *"Don't you ever play that bloody drum inside this house again!"* Off I went with my tail between my legs, and settled for my drumsticks and drum pad to show off to my mates the skills that I had learned at band practice, and boast how well I had played on the May Day Parade.

Then, one Saturday, Brian, Peter and Brendan, my schoolmates, came to see this *famous* drum, up close. I had talked my way out of going shopping with Mammy and had the house to myself. In they came, and after the normal oohs and aahs they asked me to give them a sample of my new-found talent. I explained that Mammy had told me not to play the drum in our wee house due to the racket it made, and they in turn accused me of not being able to play it properly!

47

What a *fuckin' insult!* I put on my drum sling, hooked the drum on to it and we all made our way out to our wee backyard, me thinking that the noise wouldn't travel out into the street at the front and no one would have cause to complain. Anyway, the wee backyard consisted of an outside toilet and a small shed in an area of about 25 square yards, with a wall of about 8 feet high separating us from the backyards in the houses on each side and the backyard of the house in the next street, like three sides of a square!

I began to play rudiments, then some marching beatings, and the main show-off stunt was a series of single taps played extremely quickly, five at a time, six, seven, eight and nine at a time; then I played that many that quickly, it was impossible to count them! The next thing I know, there are *two big RUC men (Royal Ulster Constabulary)* coming out our back door into our wee yard! All four of *us* gasped in unison, then the two big RUC men gasped in unison, then I heard Mammy screamin' her head off at the sight of the police car outside the front door and the more worrying sight of the two big RUC men in her backyard! *Holy fuck!*

When everyone calmed down one of the police officers explained that they were instructed to answer a 999 call; someone had reported the sound of *gunfire* being heard in the area of Scotch Street. I looked at Mammy, Mammy looked at me. I was sure that the policeman had just signed my death warrant! He further explained that the report could have been made by someone who was genuinely concerned, or by someone who was fed up with the noise being resonated in the area between the backs of the houses. Either way, it had sounded like it might be the real thing to him and his colleague when they arrived in their car. By this time the whole street was out, many of them milling around the police car. Some were having a nose through the front window of our house. Anyway, my three schoolmates soon scarpered, the two big RUC men left shortly after them, and I received my just reward: a fierce load of *fuckin' clouts* round the head. Mammy must have thought she was playing a *fuckin' big drum!* Thereafter my drum was never played in our wee house but kept in a wee cubby hole in the kitchen under the stairs until I needed it for band practice or otherwise. Guess what? It was worth it! I was not only the talk of the street, but the talk of the Loney and the talk of my school! *Every cloud, eh?*

Throughout those early days in the Pipe Band we were involved in street marches in support of local politicians canvassing for votes to gain a seat in either the local council at the City Hall, or as an MP at Stormont or Westminster. Our band would march in front of the open-top lorry while the *wannabees* waved and cheered the people on, and every so often would stop the parade to make a speech. It was great fun, and of course the band funds benefited from the fee we charged on each occasion. I met some well known politicians such as Harry Diamond MP, whose wife Pat was a good friend of Mammy, Gerry Fitt MP, later to become Lord Fitt, and Paddy Wilson, who was a member of the senate at Stormont.

In later years Lord Fitt was my guest of honour at a St Patrick's dinner night and we related fond memories of those days, which resulted in belly laughs and squeals of delight, enhanced by the amount of alcohol we consumed. Another Belfast man attended that particular dinner night; he was a very proud Shankill Road man called Paddy Shields. Paddy struck up a guitar and all three of us Belfast men sang *'I'll tell me ma'* which ended in rapturous applause from those seated, which numbered sixty-plus. Sadly, all three of those politicians have passed away.

So, as you can gather, I was kept very busy in my spare time, so much so that I bought myself a small business diary. There was so much going on, what with drama class nights, Debating Society nights, choir practice, band practice, altar boy duties, singing some Saturday afternoons at the Plaza Dancehall for the ten to fourteen year olds' dance and, lo and behold, I had to try and squeeze some homework in! All this activity, though most enjoyable, had its perks, and sometimes this would include money. The various things I had committed myself to were beginning to mount up, thus the reason for the business diary. I didn't want to double-book myself and let someone down. These days the term for double-booking oneself is, I believe, a *diary clash. OK, yah!*

While I was doing my own thing I couldn't help but realise, that the unemployment in many areas of Belfast was 20% and at times even higher. There were married couples in our street with kids older and younger than me and these parents had worked very little in their lives: one of the main reasons for moving to London, or further afield, for many Belfast people. I was determined to make my own way in life, give Mammy a few bob, have a few bob in my own pocket, and at the age of almost thirteen I was up and running, almost completely self-contained! If I overstretched myself occasionally, then so be it.

I remember listening to a young dad, who had just finished playing a game of cards at the corner of our street, and he said, *"I can't be bothered with all this runnin' around, goin' here, goin' there. I have me wee house in me wee street and as long as I have me* fegs, *and me wee* bet, *and me wee* drink *now and again. If it was good enough for* my farar, *then it's good enough for* me."

Everything in that man's life was *fuckin' wee*, he probably had a *wee dick* as well! He honestly believed that the words he had spoken had been words of:

Absolute wisdom… absolute shite, more like!

PART 2
BECOMING A TEENAGER

CHAPTER 1

WITH MY THIRTEENTH BIRTHDAY FAST APPROACHING, PREPARA-TIONS for my birthday party were well under way by the end of October 1966. I was about to become a *teenager!* By the time December 15th *(my birthday)* came along, Mammy had agreed that she and my stepfather Paddy would make themselves scarce from seven o'clock until about midnight. How great was that?

Being very aware of the rules of our house and not having been allowed to have friends in at night without Mammy or Paddy being there, I was very wary about screwing up my new-found trust! I had not tasted the delights of alcohol in any great proportion since all those years earlier with Tony and Séamus, when we celebrated our win at the talent competition. However, I honestly believed that if I was very careful, to dabble slightly on this occasion would definitely impress the *wee dolls* who were coming to my birthday party.

Bearing in mind our wee house was exactly that, *wee*, I thought it would be a good idea not to invite too many friends for this great occasion so needless to say the Gang of Four, namely Brian and Peter McAlesse, Brendan Baxter and I, would be enough manpower. With six wee dolls invited, it should be a great night!

When we four boys met a week or so prior to the party we decided to pool our money to buy a few bottles of Carling Black Label and some loose Benson and Hedges cigarettes. The *fegs* were no problem for in those days none of the local shop owners gave a monkey's shite how old you were; smokers were aged between nine and ninety! The only problem we had was getting someone to buy the beer for us from the off-licence at one of the local pubs. They would have to be over eighteen years of age, trustworthy *(we didn't want them fuckin' off with the money or fuckin' off with the beer once it had been paid for)* and also be able to keep our secret of having the beer in the first place! What a *dilemma!* We all racked our brains to come up with a suitable candidate. Then out of the blue, it hit me like a fuckin' rocket!

There was this young fella called Benny McCauley who lived in English Street, which was only two streets away from our street. Now, he was about sixteen and definitely not the *full shillin'* but his Da would send him to Doyle's Pub, which was on the corner of the same street and Cullingtree Road, to pick up a carry-out several times a week, depending how much he had won or lost on the horses. Although Benny was under age he looked older, and this transaction was always allowed to take place because Mr McCauley was pretty much confined to the house and Benny was his only means for minor purchases at the local shops *(courtesy of Séan and Bernard Brannigan, brothers of Pat, my form teacher),* putting a few bets on *(courtesy of the bookie)* and of course the carry-outs *(courtesy of Mr Doyle).*

I explained to my conspirators the devious plot I had in mind and we all agreed that Benny would be the best plan of action. We would just give him enough to get a packet of Tayto cheese and onion for carrying out the task, pat him on the back, and he would be more than pleased. *Ho Ho Ho, I'm yer fuckin' man!*

The great day in question finally arrived, the sandwiches were made, the cream buns and birthday cake had been bought from the local bakery, the two crates containing big bottles of lemonade, orange and Coke were delivered, and last but not least, I went to meet up with Benny who I had already briefed the day before. He was definitely up for it, not just for the packet of Tayto but more so for being included in this secret undercover plan. He had become part of the gang *(fuckin' eejit!)*.

I told Benny to meet me on Cullingtree Road, just down the street from Doyle's Pub and out of sight from his own house and the neighbours in English Street. We agreed to meet at a quarter past seven. Mammy and Paddy would have left our house by then, my three mates would have already arrived (Brian with the *fegs*), and the six wee dolls would be expected at just after half past seven. Everything went like clockwork and in no time at all I was back in our house with ten bottles of beer, with the wee dolls arriving shortly after. With ten of us in the wee front sitting room it was easy to get more than comfortable with all of the girls (we daren't call them *wee dolls* to their faces). One of the girls asked why there were more girls than boys and I told her that two of my mates hadn't turned up *(that seemed to do the trick)*. As the night wore on the record player was certainly the making of the party with the music getting louder and all of us having a great time, with plenty to eat and drink and the Benson and Hedges King Size Cigarettes hanging out of our gobs! Eventually I produced the bottles of beer to the delight of all present and once again the party took off to another level. The night was still but young and I was certainly glad that I had become a *teenager!*

At about half past nine a loud knock came to the door! I thought it might be one of the neighbours, possibly to complain. I turned the music down slightly, placed my *feg* into an ashtray, made my way into our wee hall, making sure that I closed the wee sitting room door behind me, gently opened the front door, peered meekly through the small gap into the street, and there he stood with a big smile on his face, *fuckin' Benny!*

"What te fuck *do you want?"* says I.

"I've come to join the party," says Benny. *"And if you don't let me in I'll go round to Doyle's Pub where yer* ma *and* da *is and tell them yer* drinkin' *an'* fuckin' smokin'*!"*

Without further ado, Benny pushed the door open, which in turn caused me to fall back onto the stairs, and he swaggered into the wee sitting room as if it was *his fuckin' birthday party!* Everyone looked round wondering who he was, until out of his trouser pocket he produced a small screwtop bottle filled with a light brown liquid.

"Anybody want a wee taste?" says Benny.

I quickly closed both the front and sitting room doors and asked what was in the bottle.

"It's whiskey!" says Benny.

"Where did ye git it?" says I.

"Sure, I take a wee bit at a time when me da has some in the house. He always gets some with his carry-out when he's a wee bit flush from winnin' on the horses. Do ya want some or not?"

Us four boys, trying very hard not to let ourselves down in front of the girls, decided to try a swig but I insisted that Benny lead the way by taking the first swallow. Benny removed the screwtop from the bottle, took what I thought was an unmerciful swig and stood there like the *big fella* in the *wee picture!* Everyone in the room was aghast at this manly feat so, like lambs to the slaughter we four boys followed suit, ensuring that we all took what appeared to be a big swig each, but in reality only took a minute amount into our mouths.

To say it blew the *fuckin' heads off us* was definitely an understatement! It wasn't long before we all started singing, girls included, what a racket! There was this wee song that I had made up in music class at school, just for a wee laugh, so I got everyone to join in with the chorus. It went to the tune of *Oh Susannah* and the words were something like this:

'The Pope's in his pyjamas and the Queen sat on his knee,
He's got a great big hard-on now, as anyone can see.
Oh, dear Lizzy, don't you cry for me,
I am the Pope, I am no dope and you sat on my knee. Oye!'

What a carry on, we couldn't stop laughing and the craic was ninety!

The music was turned up on the record player, we all started dancing again, but Benny was beginning to get a lot more attention off some of the girls than I was happy with. He was taller and older than the rest of us with a wee bit of growth on his face, which the girls found slightly more attractive than the Gang of Four!

The lights were now turned down low, a slow selection of records was placed on the record player, and Benny was having a smoochy dance with one of the girls, hands everywhere, including *hers!* When that particular record finished Benny turned to me for another bottle of beer to wash down another swig of whiskey he had just taken. The light from the kitchen showed a bulge in the front of Benny's trousers and I thought to myself *'He's got another wee bottle of whiskey and he's holding out on us'.*

I took Benny to one side and challenged him about the other wee bottle of whiskey he was hiding, to which he replied, *"Fuck ye, it's me hosepipe, ya dopey bollix!"*

At this point two of the girls pushed Benny into the wee kitchen, made their way with him to the armchair in the corner, and took up residence for what I surmised was to be for the foreseeable future!

I returned to the wee sitting room where the party was in full flow, thinking to myself *'Good idea to invite six wee dolls'.* There was still enough left for the Gang of Four. A wee while later I noticed that the main light in the kitchen was turned off, so I decided to have a wee *juke* to see what Benny and the two girls were up to. Although it was quite dark in the wee kitchen, I drew back the curtain that covered the entrance that joined with the wee sitting room, and there was just enough light from the wee sitting room to focus on the scene in the wee kitchen. At first I thought I was imagining things. There they were, all entwined on the armchair, with *Benny's hosepipe*, which must have been at least a *foot* long, standing upright like a huge dark red torch with the bulb on the outside!

Both girls had both pair of hands attached to Benny's monster and all three were oohing and aahing with delight.

I thought to myself *'The jammy **bastard**, he doesn't need a zip to keep that thing in his trousers, he needs a **fuckin' steel shutter!**'*

Anyway, I left them to it and before long it was almost midnight, time to clean the place up, get rid of any incriminating evidence, open the front and back doors to allow fresh air through the house, and send everyone on their merry way. It was a great party and a great introduction to my teenage years. My estimation of Benny went through the roof! He gave the two wee dolls more than just the average *bird bath* in our wee kitchen; he walked both of them home and by all accounts, spent a long period of time saying goodnight! Needless to say, when Mammy and Paddy came home a wee while later, I disguised my alcohol-induced breath with a trick I had picked up from Tony and Séamus years earlier, by chewing lots of Polo Mints! I said that we had a great time, that everyone had behaved themselves and with that, I said my goodnights and went off to bed, like the good *wee crater* Mammy said I was!

Christmas and New Year were soon to follow and went equally as well for me as my birthday party. It was strange being a teenager, I sort of felt that I was beginning to grow up, and I also felt almost ready for the new term at school; dare I say it, almost looking forward to it!

CHAPTER 2

1967 STARTED OFF WITH A HECTIC SCHEDULE. The drama teacher, Pat Brannigan, had informed us that we were ready to perform a production on stage, in front of a real live audience! The play he had chosen was written by J. M. Synge, entitled *The Playboy of the Western World*. Auditions for various characters took place over a couple of weeks, with yours truly being designated as the lead male role, Christy Mahon, the said playboy in the title.

The work rate of Pat Brannigan and other members of the school teaching staff was phenomenal! It was the first serious attempt by St Gabriel's School to undertake such a challenge in the world of amateur dramatics.

The girls required for the play were supplied by volunteers from an all-girls' school, just up the road from St Gabriel's, called Our Lady of Mercy. I thought, with a school with a name like that, the girls in question would be all holier-than-thou and probably be *pigs in knickers!* We were all in for a pleasant surprise. All the girls were nice to look at and even nicer to talk to, with all the cast members, stage hands, general helpers and sweeper-uppers, taking the whole thing very seriously indeed!

Meanwhile, at the first band practice of the new year, Séan Dillon, the pipe major, informed us all that St Mary's Pipe Band would be taking part in competitions throughout the coming year and we were also committed to quite a few music festivals, parades and indoor private functions! This meant that the band would be travelling a lot more throughout the whole of Ireland, and our playing would need to raise its standard to a much higher level! PHEW!

The Debating Society was still in full flow and Mr Jones *(still can't remember the wee shite's first name who was our French teacher)*, had been put in charge because we were about to travel around Belfast to other school debating societies in the coming term, with a view, if we behaved ourselves, that these excursions would become a permanent fixture for the coming year. The visits would include not only boys' schools but girls' schools and mixed schools as well. I quite liked the sound of that, simply because I was taking more than just a wee interest in the opposite sex!

Although I still loved to sing with the choir, Mr Moore, *(the vice-principal, who was also our music teacher)*, remained very solemn and formal throughout our rehearsals, so I thought I would opt for a change to the newly formed Folk Club. The Folk Club always met at night and was open to anyone interested from any other school in the local area, which included Our Lady of Mercy Girls' School! If anyone interested could sing, play an instrument, clap their hands or make an acceptable sound of any sort, they were more than welcome. Michael Tanney *(can't remember what subject he taught)*, who was also very much involved with Pat Brannigan in the Dramatic Society, was the mainstay of the club and extremely handy on the guitar.

Altar boy duties were looking pretty good, however: a lot of the weddings were booked for the summer, when most of the pipe band competitions were being held, so I had to scrutinise the dates in both cases!

Singing at the Plaza Dance Hall on the odd Saturday afternoon was still on the cards so it was time to get myself another business diary!

Sometime in the coming year the redevelopment of the Loney began. At first a lot of the community were in awe of the amount of workmen *(some, but not a lot, from the local area),* the amount of machinery, bulldozers and such like, and the huge and sometimes majestic cranes that appeared. Most of the heavy equipment remained in situ throughout the redevelopment period, which was to last for more than five years. After only a few months a strange occurrence began to take place: a very high rise in the deaths of senior citizens! They were dropping like flies; it seemed to be one or two per week! It was investigated quite quickly by the local powers-that-be and the theory they came up with was as follows.

The older generation of the Loney had mentally decided that they would rather die in their wee houses *(in some cases, hovels)* than watch them being knocked down, and then move into a modern maisonette/flat system where they could easily be forgotten, and have little or no independence, even with the new-fangled lifts that would, more often than not, be out of order or absolutely frightening to use. They felt they would be almost prisoners in their new homes!

Gone would be the *oul* cooker in the corner, replaced by some space age contraption; gone would be the *oul* coal fire, replaced by central heating that would be almost impossible to operate, with that peculiar dial on the wall; out with the old, in with the new whether it suited or not! It was a crying shame but the days of the Pound Loney were, for all the right reasons, well and truly over!

As new dwellings went up, old ones came down, families began to move into the warren of maisonettes, and eventually it was our turn to leave our wee house in Scotch Street to occupy our *brand new flat* in Divis Tower! There were twenty floors in Divis Tower with five flats on each floor, a mixture of one and two bedrooms. Mammy, Paddy and I took up residence in a two-bedroom flat on the eleventh floor, 11E. I remember looking out over the new estate and I had to admit that, at a distance, it all looked very grand and well-finished, but it could also be the birth of a concrete jungle!

Divis Tower was everything the public relations people had said it would be and everything the oul folk had worried about. Most of the tenants were elderly, a few were middle-aged and I was the only teenager living there. Most of the tenants on the upper floors, from the tenth upwards, got the shock of their lives when they looked out of their windows!

"A lovely view of Belfast," said the female housing rep. Lovely my *arse!* Even I had to stand back from our window initially because of the distance from the ground, and our flat was only just over halfway up.

A majority of tenants had little or no confidence in the two lifts, which on entry to the main entrance hall were found on either side of the hall. One of them stopped at the even-numbered floors, and the other one stopped at the odd-numbered floors. Although there were two lift shafts, there was only one lift access on each floor. Therefore, if you lived on an evennumbered floor and the lift wasn't working or you got fed up waiting, you had to get the other lift, get off at the next oddnumbered floor above yours and walk down two flights of stairs to your final destination! Likewise, if the situation was reversed! Nice and easy for the elderly clientele, *not!*

The cookers were fine according to Mammy but I had to agree with the worriers from the oul Loney: the central heating was never totally satisfactory. It was either *too* warm or *too* cold and along with the big hike in rent it was, without doubt, *too* expensive!

After the unfortunate experience of the old and bold dying off at the start of the redevelopment, now they were worrying themselves to death because their income was being depleted each week with devastating effect! What in *God's* name was anyone in authority going to do about it?

Apart from the female housing rep or her male pimply-faced partner in crime *(because what was happening to these senior citizens was a fuckin' **crime!**)*, no-one gave a *monkey's fuck!*

Shortly after all the flats were full the first of the elderly tenants died. *Surprise! Surprise!*

Getting people in and out for the wake was an absolute nightmare, and how the undertakers got the oul fella up to the fourteenth floor in the lift, with the deceased inside the upright coffin and without him falling out, was nothing short of a miracle! I was present for the removal of his remains to St Peter's Cathedral, and I've got to say of the scenario that took place, you couldn't make it up! Little did I realise, in later years, how much of a sought-after authority I would become in such matters!

But, as they say, life must go on. Needless to say, not long after we settled into our new flat, the Gang of Four from school made their first visit. I've got to say that I was pleasantly surprised that on that initial visit and subsequent visits we managed to stay out of trouble within the confines of Divis Tower for which Mammy and Paddy were very grateful. It may have had something to do with the ultimatum that Mammy gave us on that memorable first occasion: *"There'll be three families missin' childer if yuse don't bloody behave yerselves in this block o' flats!"* Oh, Mammy, you certainly had a way with words.

With Paddy's Day followed by Easter, the Pipe Band was up and running well with band practices on Wednesday nights and Sunday afternoons. We were booked to play at quite a few parties and parades and our standard of playing and deportment were improving all the time, but still not good enough for the forthcoming competition

63

season as we were all reminded of, on many occasions, by our Pipe Major, Séan Dillon. His brother Eamonn as leading drummer tried very hard but, as I said earlier, he started late in life as a pipe band side-drummer and therefore there was only a certain amount of ground he was capable of covering, although I've got to say if there was ever a prize for determination he would win it every time! But help was soon to be on its way.

The Dramatic Society was really taking off with our first production *The Playboy of the Western World*, with rehearsals being twice a week (Tuesday and Thursday nights), with everyone turning up on time and willing to stay late if necessary. Pat Brannigan had given us all a target to be achieved before the Easter holidays and we were all committed to achieving it!

Altar boy duties and performing at the Plaza on Saturday afternoons were going nicely, but I knew with the pipe band competition season coming up in the summer something would have to give! The Debating Society for a start; well, only if I had to!

The Folk Club was on Monday nights; that left Friday nights for the pictures and Saturday nights for the Gang of Four to meet up in one of our homes to sing, play records or, if we were lucky enough, get invited to a party. With the new acquaintances we were making at the Folk Club and the Dramatic Society, plus the fact we could give a good oul rendition of song and dance combined with a bit of comedy, *fuck me, we were elected!*

Sunday nights were always spent at home. I think it may have had something to do with *exhaustion!* Anyway, Mammy said I wasn't allowed out *seven* nights a bloody week!

CHAPTER 3

D URING EASTER WEEK, FOR WHATEVER REASON, MAMMY was a
bit flush, and although she had mentioned to me earlier in
the year that we may get the chance for a return visit to
London, I couldn't believe my ears when she announced that we were
going to London for a week! On this journey, however, we would be
flyin'! Fuckin' *great!* My stepfather Paddy would not be able to come
due to work commitments, so Mammy and I packed our bags and the
very next day we were on our way to the bus station at Great Victoria
Street to catch the bus to the *airport! Ho ho fuckin' ho*, another *taxi*
ride, this time watched by the newly-built complex of Divis Tower
and Divis Maisonettes. I was even waving at the neighbours as if I
was part of some sort of royal cavalcade!

When I asked Mammy how we could afford to fly to London,
she explained that we would get a standby flight. In those days you
could turn up at the airport, put your name down at the relevant desk,
and when your name was called out you simply went up to the same
desk and paid the princely sum of £3 for a one-way ticket to London.
How simple is that? Mammy also explained that sometimes the wait
to be called forward may be quite a while, thus the reason for our
sandwiches and lemonade. However, I watched her use the same
Belfast charm she had used on the Heysham boat on our last trip to
London: *"I'm just a wee woman with my wee son goin' te London for
a funeral."*

I nearly started laughing and had to say that I needed to go to the toilet. I was so glad I didn't have to listen to the remainder of Mammy's story, and by the time I came back Mammy whispered, *"Luck as if yer goin' te cry. Hurry up or I'll give ya somethin' te cry fer!"*

With that instruction in mind I put in one of my finest performances; not to overdo it, just enough for Mammy to put her arms around me. She looked down at me and there was a slight tear beginning to fall from both eyes. She whispered, *"I was only codin' ye on son. I wasn't really goin' te make ye cry."* What Mammy didn't realise was that I could cry at *will!* Something I discovered at a very early age, and since attending the Dramatic Society had perfected to an *art form!*

Anyway, after about an hour or so our names were called out and we went to the desk and got our tickets and handed in our luggage. There would be another short wait before we would be allowed to board the plane and I couldn't wait! I thought to myself *'What's the Gang of Four and the rest of me schoolmates goin' te say when I tell them this one?'*

When our seat numbers were called out, we walked the short distance from the terminal across the tarmac to the waiting shiny white plane, with two propellered engines on each wing. Along the side of the main body of the aircraft in huge capital letters were the words *British European Airways* (BEA).

The whole experience of boarding the plane and taking our seats was unbelievable; me inside a real airplane and actually going to fly to London in it and then getting a seat next to the window; fuckin' *great!* It was when I settled into my seat that I took in the view presented to me through the small window, where I noticed a large sign that read: ***Nutts Corner***.

I began to feel just a hint of panic setting in and I mouthed the following words without making a sound.

"Holy fuck, is that what the fuckin' airport's called? Nutts – fuckin' – Corner?"

Another act of contrition sprang to mind but I managed not to show my concern to Mammy or any of the cabin crew. Thank God there was nobody in the outside seat of our row to witness my plight. If I took a deep breath, everything would be *OK!* The cavalry arrived in the shape of the comedy act that was to follow: the cabin crew pre-flight routine of safety procedures and demonstration of emergency equipment. All three cabin crew were girls, well, two girls and a *gorilla*. The two girls were very pretty and their uniforms fitted them perfectly but it was very obvious that one of them was a wee bit nervous. This particular fact did me no good whatsoever! I think it was her first trip as a fully trained crew member, and the fact that the gorilla, who was in charge, looked like she was chewing a fuckin' *wasp!*

Well, let me tell you this, after the initial welcome on board by the captain, Godzilla the Gorilla took control of a small handset and began her commentary. We were seated about halfway down the cabin and could see the slightly nervous one of the two girls, who was quite close to us. If I stretched and crooked my neck a wee bit, I could see Godzilla's head just above the seats in front of me. When the commentary began, well, I thought Mammy was going to wet herself, such was the phoney accent that Godzilla was using, to obviously impress the more seasoned passengers on board.

Anyway, there were hands pointing here, there were hands pointing there, here, there and everywhere, throw your knickers in the air! And with Godzilla's tongue shooting from one side of her mouth to the other, then out, then in, I was waiting for someone to produce a fuckin' *rabbit* out of a fucking *hat!* Then came the *piece de resistance*:

the fitting of the individual life jackets. Our demonstrator was very capable of putting the life jacket on, but unfortunately she had tied the strap around her waist so tight she couldn't undo it to carry on with the demonstration of the oxygen masks, should it be necessary for them to be released from above our heads. By this stage Godzilla was just about to have a fuckin' *calf*, when she forgot where she was and the posh accent changed briefly to that of a Belfast paper-boy!

Almost immediately she corrected herself. At this stage Mammy was definitely out of control, as were most of the other passengers, and the wee girl who was having all the trouble with the life jacket was sweating like a mad dog trying to shag his shadow! Once every-body settled down and everything was how it should be, I could feel the plane going backwards. Godzilla and the two girls had already handed out sweets to suck during takeoff to stop our ears popping. It crossed my mind that although the cabin crew had covered what was considered to be all emergency situations, they didn't say anything about an emergency over dry land so I asked Mammy where the parachutes were kept. She gave me a clip round the ear and told me not to be so smart. *I only fuckin' asked!*

By the time we were ready for takeoff, it was early evening and dusk was edging its way across the airport. When the captain finally let rip, I held on to my seat for dear life and purposely did not look out of the window! After only a few moments I relented and gradually turned to the small window, and I honestly couldn't believe my eyes. Belfast and the surrounding area looked absolutely, unbelievably beautiful, with the sun beginning to fade and all the flickering lights below, with a number of small white clouds that looked like champ potatoes! My belly was rumbling; what with all the excitement I was getting hungry. It wasn't long before the plane levelled out and the two girls were dishing out hot snacks with hot or cold drinks, served right up to our seats! *Fuckin' great!* Mammy and I had some sort of fish pie and a can of Coke. I couldn't believe how little food was in each tray and the cans of Coke were absolutely miniscule! If the captain was getting the same grub I only hoped he would have the strength to get us to London and land safely!

After about half an hour the captain announced that we were passing over Liverpool or somewhere like that and then after another half hour or so, he announced we were approaching London Heathrow. This time there would be no hesitation in looking out of the window and I sat goggle eyed at the sight that unfolded beneath us. I began to make out the motorways and main roads, then some buildings, then some houses, all far below, all visible because of the vast array of lights in every direction. It reminded me of some sort of sci-fi film I had seen recently in the Clonard Cinema: *Flash Gordon* I think it was, but only on a much larger scale! I have to admit that just before the plane touched down I closed my eyes and once again held on for dear life. I was so glad when the plane pulled into its stand and I finally realised we were down in one piece. As we were leaving the plane Godzilla was at the front door beside the steps, smiling and waving and wishing everyone a safe onward journey, speaking once again as if she had *piles* in her *gub!* When Mammy and I got close to her, I could see that she was quite a bit older than the other two girls of the cabin crew and her face was caked in a light tan spread of makeup; it must have been at least an inch thick! Her lipstick was even redder and thicker up close than I could have imagined. If she gave somebody a kiss it would look like they needed a blood transfusion! As we made our way down the steps Mammy said, *"Her man must be a plasterer. Her makeup was put on with a bloody trowel!"*

When we collected our luggage we made our way to Arrivals and met up with Billy. He gave Mammy a big kiss and me a fuckin' bear hug! We were soon on the Tube and on our way to stay with Billy and his wife Tish and their family, near the centre of London. I fell fast asleep within only a few moments of entering the Tube train, a habit I became famous for in years to come, when someone said that I could sleep on a fuckin' *washin' line!*

The next week was spent visiting friends and relatives, namely the Quinn family who originally came from Belfast and Cookstown: Monica and Ted, Gerry and Jo, and I think Frank and Maura. With the weather as great as it was, some more sightseeing, all in all a fantastic way to spend time over the Easter holidays. On our return to Belfast via another standby flight with BEA, I had a few more fantastic tales to tell in the Divis, the Gang of Four and all me other mates at school; oh yes, and the Pipe Band and the Dramatic Society and the Folk Club. I particularly liked the reaction I got from the girls on every occasion! *Did I put the 'ooo' in 'smoooth', or what?*

CHAPTER 4

B ACK TO SCHOOL FOR THE SUMMER TERM was the start of another round of scrapes and near misses with regards to being found out when the Gang of Four were up to no good. However, my altar boy days were about to come to an abrupt end! On a visit to Brian and Peter's Granny's house, which was quite close to Ligoniel Church where our altar boy duties took place, we were kicking a football around when the other Brendan kicked the ball away into the air and into the church grounds. Although it was still quite bright, it was about eight o'clock and the front gates were very rarely locked. When we were looking for the ball we noticed that the front main doors of the church were locked, but on further investigation found the small side door leading into the room adjacent to the main altar was slightly ajar. All four of us, Peter carrying the ball, made our way inside calling out to find out if anyone was there. Brian switched on the light and we realised we were in the vestry. We had a quick look into the main building of the church, but as there were no lights on and it was beginning to get darker and eerier by the second, we made our way back to the vestry.

Being our normal inquisitive selves, we had a wee poke around and noticed a long, unusually-shaped key on the window sill. Peter and I were discussing what it could be for; at this stage, the other Brendan was helping Brian to try on one of the priests' vestments! Brian really looked the part even though the garments were a bit

71

on the big size, but when Brendan shoved the football up the back of the cassock, Brian gave a great impression of *Quasimodo, The Hunchback Of Notre Dame!*

We all burst out laughing, and the more we tried to stop, the more we kept on laughing. We were all signalling to each other to shush with one finger over our mouths, but the tears were now taking over and the squawks of us trying to suppress the noise of our laughter were beginning to echo into the main building of the church. Eventually a form of sanity returned to the situation, but every so often one of us would get a fit of the giggles!

Our attention once again was on the key we found earlier. On looking round the room, none of us could determine where the key would fit until I noticed a small metal door in the wall: it was a safe! The key fitted, turned easily and the door, helped by a good tug, opened to reveal three bottles of *red wine!* We all smiled at each other and by mutual consent and nods of approval I removed the three bottles, one almost empty and the other two completely full. We tasted the wine in the open bottle first, and all four of us agreed that although it wasn't great, we could get used to it, which prompted me to open one of the other two bottles but we had a slight problem: how do we get the cork out? The cavalry arrived in the shape of Brian's new penknife which had numerous bits and pieces on it for any amount of wee jobs, and after showing off all its attributes he proudly produced a fuckin' corkscrew.

Brian very quickly pulled the cork from the bottle, and using the cups and saucers that were on the table we made use of the two old armchairs and proceeded to drink our wine. We decided to put the remaining full bottle back into the safe along with the bottle we had opened, leaving a small amount of wine in the open bottle. The priest who opened the safe the next day would assume that there was one full bottle of wine and one almost empty bottle, and hopefully be none the wiser! *Then disaster struck!* In the shape of a priest nicknamed *the grey-haired monster!*

Father McCloskey appeared in the side doorway. We four jumped to our feet, Brian tripped on the long vestments, knocking the cups from Peter and Brendan's hands and smashing them on the floor, and the football which had dislodged itself from its hunchback position on Brian's back was bouncing round the room with me chasing it! Father McCloskey began ranting and raving in Latin *(I'm sure he was cursin' and swearin').* I thought our world had come to an end! When the pandemonium was over there was absolutely nothing we could say or do to vindicate ourselves. We were well and truly in the *shite!*

When Father McCloskey finished boxing us around the ears, he stood all four of us in a line and threatened to excommunicate us from the Catholic Church. What was I going to tell Mammy? But the Brendan McCann experience was about to kick in. I turned on the tears full throttle, held my right hand over my right ear and declared that Father McCloskey had damaged my lughole with the amount of pain he had inflicted upon me. The oul priest began to panic, asked to make a more thorough inspection of the said lughole, to which I informed him it was too sore for him to touch. The other three began to clean up the mess while I went into overdrive with *me awful sore ear!*

After about ten minutes or so, the mess had been cleaned up, the remainder of the wine was back in the safe and Father McCloskey began to calm down. He began to take stock of the situation. He could call my bluff about how much pain I was in but run the risk of getting into serious trouble, or in this case decide that the punishment dished out by him would suffice and in his own words *'There'll be no more talk about it'.* All four of us were thankful for the latter but as we made our way through the church grounds, I began to mimic Father McCloskey's reaction to the scene before him when he entered the

73

changing room, and to my dismay Brian pointed out that he was right behind us! I decided there and then that my altar boy days were well and truly over.

Coming into the summer months of 1967 was the experience of the competition season with the Pipe Band. There would be six different grades throughout the season to be adjudicated, with a judge for drumming, two judges for piping, a judge for marching and discipline, and when it was a major competition *(or a well-attended gathering),* there would be a judge for ensemble. There was also a drum major's competition which was judged separately sometime throughout the day with marching music played by a designated band.

The six grades for the pipe bands would range from grade one to grade four, with the top bands playing in grade one and the less experienced or less talented bands playing two, three and four. Our band would compete in grade four. The remaining two grades were Juvenile, then Novice and Juvenile. I think these two grades speak for themselves.

As well as the twice weekly band practices, there was always a practice on the Friday night preceding the competition, and with Eamonn the leading drummer sometimes having additional drumming practice at his home. We received extra tuition for technical ability, musical content and overall performance within the drum section: bass drum, tenor drum, and of course the side-drums. This expertise was supplied by a local man called Jimmy Maguire, who wasn't competing with any particular band at this time but was using his remarkable talents to assist the likes of Eamonn and me. He assisted us on and off for about two years. What with people coming and going all the time within the band, it was sometimes an uphill struggle for all of us who stayed on to improve our performance to an acceptable standard to win something, but hey, God loves a trier!

Our first competition was in May or June in the lovely wee town of Banbridge. All outdoor competitions are held in a field of some sort which has been squared off with ticker-tape, with tents for the judges' paperwork and to provide shelter for the said judges when inclement weather prevails. There is also a starting line marked in white chalk for the front rank of the participating band to start from, and two circles, one within the other, a short distance in front of the starting line, marked out with white chalk for that band to march into and play their designated music. The band in question, when instructed to do so by one of the judges, will then, on the command of the pipe major, step off with two three-pace rolls from the drummers, form a circle, halt together at the end of a part of music which is signalled by the pipe major. Most bands, depending on their size, will halt within the inner circle , with the judges being allowed no closer to the band than the outer circle.

Let me tell you straight, it was a feat just to get into the circle and halt together, never mind play instruments at the same bloody time! Anyway, our turn came and as soon as the pipe major gave the command *"rolls, quick march!"* most of us turned into rubber men! Needless to say we didn't start too well, then we went completely down the drain until we finished our tune; well, we sort of finished at different times, instead of all together! To say that the pipe major was *spittin' fuckin' feathers* was certainly the understatement of the century! If the truth be known, most of us hid our faces from the remainder of those present, of which there were quite a few including fellow competitors, supporters and members of the general public, but in no time at all we were approached by members of a lot of other bands offering sympathy *and,* most of all, encouragement and stories of their own botched-up performances in their early days of competing. I've got to admit, I was seriously considering packing the whole thing in until Eamonn, our leading drummer, came up to me with a great big 99 ice cream and said, *"We might not have played that well but we certainly looked the part!"*

By this time Séan the pipe major had calmed down and we all agreed to try and do better next time. When we received our Piping and Drumming sheets containing our scores and the judges' comments it was like reading the fuckin' *Beano*, not just because of some of the scathing remarks but because of the poor handwriting, the poor spelling and the extremely poor fuckin' *grammar!* I thought to myself *'At least we'll improve but those ignoramuses will go to their graves as thick as fuck!'*

CHAPTER 5

THE NEXT IMPORTANT THING ON MY AGENDA was our first production of the Dramatic Society, *The Playboy of the Western World*, which was to be performed on a Friday and Saturday night towards the end of the summer term. Rehearsals were going according to plan, scenery and costumes were coming along nicely, and the whole school was *buzzin'* with anticipation, from the headmaster (Mr McGuinness) right down to the normal toerag. A lot of doubting Thomases couldn't resist a quick visit now and again to satisfy themselves that this production was really going to take place, and take place with a *bloody vengeance!*

After a lot of hard work from all concerned, our *big* chance to prove ourselves came at last! On the first of the two nights, which was Friday, the school assembly hall was packed to capacity with those unable to get seats standing along the back wall! The noise coming from the audience area and in the corridors leading to the assembly hall was exhilarating, to the point of boosting all our adrenalin to an almost uncontrollable level! Pat Brannigan called us all together *(from the lead role to the sweeper-upper),* and in his very calm but authoritative voice ran us through what happens if something goes wrong, how to rely on the prompters *(one on each side of the stage)* etc. etc., and at the end of his pep talk he said, *"Above all, go out there and enjoy yourselves!"*

I have to say at this stage, I was thinking back to my first competition with the Pipe Band, and having competed in several competitions since that sorry day I had improved considerably in that discipline. I was determined to put any nervousness out of my mind and as the leading man in the play, lead by example and put on the very best show possible.

The curtains opened and everyone took off like absolute professionals. All the props were in the right place, all the scenery looked great; everyone's make-up looked even better and *no-one* needed the assistance of either of the *prompters!* When we took our curtain call at the end of the performance, the applause was deafening and I realised, there and then, this was a great way to spend a Friday night!

Just before the start of Saturday night's performance, Pat Brannigan once again gave us our pep talk but also told us that there were even more people queuing up to get in than on the Friday night! I slipped away onto the side of the stage and peered out of the side curtain. *My God!* Once again all the seats were taken with extra seats put out wherever a space could be found. Schoolkids of all ages were sitting on the floor in the centre and side aisles and once again there were lots of people standing along the back wall!

Another great performance by all was rewarded by thunderous applause, whistles, cheers and a standing ovation at the end. When we took our curtain call, the noise only died down when Pat Brannigan walked on stage and thanked everyone for turning up to watch us. He didn't have to thank the cast; just one look from him along the line of performers and a great big smile appeared on his face, then someone shouted, *"Three cheers for St Gabriel's Dramatic Society!"* Well, you should have heard the fuckin' *roar* that went up! We all looked at each other, and knew right there and then we just had to do another play at the earliest opportunity. In Monday's edition of the *Irish News* we had a fantastic write-up with photographs as well! It gave names to accompany the photographs but one particular line written in the paper, that has remained with me to this day, was *'A stab in the arm for amateur dramatics in Belfast'!*

School summer holidays were soon to arrive and of course the school closed down, including the Dramatic Society, the Folk Club and the Debating Society, which meant I would have a lot more spare time at night than I would normally have during term time. It gave me more time during the day for what were to become my favourite sports: football and swimming, and also a lot more time for drum practice. However, although the Gang of Four still met up regularly for nights out or nights in singing and playing music, I began to venture into town a bit more often. Sometimes Brian would get the bus from Ligoniel and meet me in town. We would wander round some of the amusement arcades that were springing up all around the city centre. In those days there was probably some sort of age restriction because some of the arcades had one-armed bandits and other similar gambling machines, but as long as you behaved no one really bothered; bit like the sale of cigarettes to underage kids like Brian and me, which remained rife for many years to come!

One night we were passing a pub near the centre of town called *Kelly's Cellars* when we heard this very lively foot-tapping music coming from within. We tried to look through the window but either the glass was too thick to see through, or too thick with dirt, I'm not too sure which, so I decided to have a wee juke inside the front door to see if I could get a glimpse of what was going on, while Brian watched my back. There was a four-piece folk group playing in the far corner of the bar and it was obvious from the audience participation that everyone was in a very merry sing-song party mood. Knowing this pub to be one of many that Uncle Mick frequented when he was on one of his many walkabouts, I strolled up to the side of the bar, said a quick hello to the barman who I hoped remembered me from a previous visit with Uncle Mick, and casual as you like enquired if the said man had been in that night as he told me to meet him there but I was a wee bit late. The barman told me that Uncle Mick had in fact left about a half an hour before but if I wanted to wait for a wee while in case he came back, I could sit in the corner out of the way. I thanked him for his kindness and asked if my cousin who was waiting outside could join me. I also added that my cousin was a year older than me and that we would be *no trouble at all!* The barman thought for a moment, then he agreed; then he said he would be *"kape-in a close eye on yis!"*

Anyway, much to Brian's surprise, he and I sat down at a table in the corner and the party atmosphere was fantastic, with the folk group playing two guitars, a banjo and a tin whistle; they weren't bad singers either. The barman and his assistant *(an oul fella about ninety years of age!)* became very busy, rushed off their feet in fact, and forgot all about us in the corner, so we were going to be there for quite some time. Brian suggested going to the bar for a glass of fizzy orange to which I replied, *"Fuck me, Brian, not fuckin' fizzy orange. I have an idea, get two glasses of Coke instead."* Brian duly carried out my request, making sure he approached the oul fella behind the bar, who didn't know what day it was, never mind that we were making ourselves at home! When Brian returned to *our* table we quickly drank one of the glasses of Coke and kept the empty glass close to hand. There were two tables to our right and one to our left, quite close to the gents' toilets. Now, just about everybody was drinking stout or some sort of dark bitter, some had draught, some had bottles but in the lowly-lit bar area, with cigarette and pipe smoke hanging in the air, it all looked pretty much the same, especially if you were well-oiled. My plan was as follows: as soon as one of the drinkers from the tables closest to us went to the bogs, Brian or I would start up a conversation with whoever else was sitting there, thus providing a slight distraction and an opportunity to procure some drink from the drinker's glass who was now in the bogs having a slash, by pouring the drink (not too much, now) into our empty Coke glass! Brian thought that this was a great idea and couldn't wait to get started.

Well, let me tell you, it went like a fuckin'*dream!* None of the drinkers closest to us had a clue what was going on; one of them even bought us each a half pint of Guinness as a reward for joining in the singing *and* for singing so well! As the night wore on, the drinker that bought us the Guinness came back from the bar, with a glass of what appeared to be Coke. He told us it was a double *vodka* and Coke, set it on the table and proceeded to the toilet. Brian and I just looked at each other and we simply couldn't resist the temptation that was before us. At this stage, because just about everyone in the pub was drunk, we didn't even bother to strike up a diversionary conversation to conceal the theft of the wee man's drink, we just drank most of it between us and poured some of our flat Coke into his glass! The wee man returned to the table, lashed the *vodka* down in one, shook his head, walked up to the oul fella behind the bar and accused him of serving short measures!

Brian and I decided it was time to go home. *Jesus Christ!* As soon as we hit the fresh air, we began to stagger slightly, then we started laughing, then Brian let rip with this great big *fart!* I followed suit and nearly *followed through!* Then the *hiccups* kicked in! We both started taking deep breaths and Brian nearly choked to death which inevitably sent me into another ruction of laughter! Eventually we sort of came to our senses, Brian got the bus home, and it took me forever to walk the short distance from Castle Street to Divis Flats. I don't remember much about arriving home, I just shouted to Mammy that I was in and going to bed. Thankfully she and Paddy were watching something on telly and didn't come to check on me until sometime later. Brian wasn't so lucky. He fell asleep upstairs on the bus and when the bus completed its return journey to Belfast city centre, Brian was still on it! *And guess what?* It was the last bus to Ligoniel that night! Needless to say, Brian had a long walk home with an even longer explanation to his parents as to why he was so late getting home.

One Saturday afternoon, after I finished my spot at the Plaza dance hall, I asked the man in charge of the wee trio *(two guitarists and a drummer)* who accompanied the singers if I could stay behind and have a go on the drums. I knew that they would leave their gear on stage as the trio would be joined by four others to play for the adult dance *(sixteens and over)*, on Saturday nights. He checked with the manager whose name was Brian Ferry *(not **the** Brian Ferry)*, and because Brian knew me not just from singing in the Plaza but also from my days of living in the Pound Loney (as he had lived in English Street, just two streets away from where we used to live) he kindly agreed. Apart from staff setting up the place for the Saturday night dance there was only me and the resident drummer on stage, whose name was Davey Baker. Now, Davey knew that I played a drum in a pipe band, but he was slightly worried about how much I didn't know about a set of drums, with all the bits and pieces that go with them and even more worried about how much damage I would do to *his* drums, which after all played a major part of *his* livelihood. Anyway, Davey kindly took me through a few basic rudimental rhythms pertaining to a set of drums, and was quite surprised how quickly I picked up the stick movement; however, at this stage I hadn't realised that I was also required to move my right foot to activate the pedal for the bass drum and my left foot to activate the pedal for the double set of cymbals known as the hi-hat! Then the *fucker* told me to incorporate the two tom-toms attached to the top of the bass drum, and when I was completely confused he told me to hit the tenor bass drum situated immediately to my right!

Well, I have to say, I may as well have been playing *Hands Knees and Bumps A Daisies!* Davey was trying very hard not to laugh but he failed; *miserably!* I think Davey was under the misconception that if he gave me enough rope, I would get fed up and not bother him any more. *Big fuckin' mistake!* The more frustrated I became, the more determined I was to get it right, so Davey left me to my own devices for an hour or so, and on his return he was surprised that although I was still playing the snare drum, I wasn't playing any of the other percussion pieces. *"Now now,"* he said, *"if you want to become a proper drummer, you have to be able to play all the rhythms on all of the kit."* To which I replied, *"Davey, one bit of kit at a time."* We both laughed and soon I was on my way home with a devious plan up my sleeve.

When I next had our flat to myself, I organised a few bits and pieces in my room in a makeshift formation of a drum set. I took a small, armless, wooden-backed chair and placed my practice drum pad in the centre of the seat *(snare drum)*, draped two tea towels over the back to prevent any damage *(two tom-toms),* placed my laundry bin with plastic lid on my righ *(tenor bass).* I then proceeded to practise the rhythms that Davey had shown me, making sure that I was moving around my makeshift drums a wee bit at a time. When it was time to give my hands a rest, I practised with firstly my right foot to achieve a solid sound from the floor *(bass drum)* and then my left foot to represent the double cymbals *(hi-hat).* I practised in this mode as often as Mammy and Paddy would allow. It was a long hard process, but by the following Saturday, after the normal afternoon session at the Plaza, Davey stood in utter amazement at the progress I had made, and I wasn't backward about being forward in letting him know that by giving me that first lesson the previous week, he had made a cross for his own back! After a few weeks of pleading with Davey *(which I was exceptionally good at)*, we got the *OK* for me to stay until the full band *(seven in all)* arrived for their sound check and just, just, just maybe *'have a wee go with them.'*

Anyway, when all seven of the band were ready for their sound check, I stood on the dance floor immediately in front of the stage. The trio of two guitarists and drummer were joined by another guitarist, an organist and two saxophone players. What an impressive-looking line-up! Well, when they started playing I couldn't believe the sound, and the vocals, especially with the harmonies, were absolutely fantastic!

After a wee while the lead guitarist (Big Willy) invited me to join them on stage and I suddenly became speechless and suffered temporary paralysis! I finally got behind the drums, and with an additional two cymbals added *(suspended on stands, one each side of the tom-toms)*, I felt as if all my Christmases had come at once! We started playing a few intros at first, then a few bars, then a few lines of a song and then a complete tune. There was me playing at the sound check with the resident band at the Plaza, whose posters were all over the dance hall and on billboards around Belfast. Yes, folks, I was playing with the famous Ferrymen Showband *(well, they were famous enough for me!)*. When the sound check was over, Big Willy and the rest of the band invited me back as often as possible on future Saturday afternoons to have another wee go! I rushed home to tell Mammy and Paddy, and rushed even more to meet up with the Gang of Four to tell them of my new-found status.

A few months later, after many Saturday sessions with the Ferrymen and in between pipe band competitions, Davey Baker took me to one side and told me of a talent competition to be held in the Plaza. He also told me that all contestants had to be over sixteen years of age. Now, although there would be the odd act that would slip through the net and be younger than sixteen, it would be a definite *no-no* for me to try to get my name on the list of contestants. However, Brian Ferry and the Ferrymen agreed that if I was up to the mark, I could join the band on stage on the night to play the drums in two, or possibly three of the tunes in their programme. Even before Davey had finished speaking I could visualise my name up in lights: *For One Night Only It's Brendan And His Ferrymen!*

Once my feet came back to ground level, two tunes were selected with a third in reserve. Over the next few weeks I practised with the band on Saturday afternoons, at home on my makeshift drum set, and with all the extra practice I was getting with the Pipe Band, my wrists were becoming exceptionally flexible, with my sense of rhythm and timing improving to a standard that impressed Eamonn in the Pipe Band, and Davey in the Show Band!

Eventually the big night arrived and Mammy was fussing all over me. Now, the show band always wore bright-coloured suits with frilly shirts and bow ties so, although I had the recommended well-pressed black trousers, black shoes and socks, whiter-than-white shirt and bow tie, Mammy in her wisdom didn't want me to be the odd one out so, from God knows where, she got me an attachable black and white frilly bit to go on the front of my shirt! Mammy duly fitted the frilly bit to the buttons of my shirt, and with the nice new bow tie to set it off she cooed, *"Look at my wee boy, all dickied up with his wee dickie bow."* Fuck me! I thought, I looked like a *wee fruit!*

Anyway, off I went down through the Divis Flats with me hair all slicked back and making sure that, although it was a very warm summer's evening, my duffle coat was done up all the way to the top button, ensuring that no one could see the frilly bit and dickie bow that Mammy was so proud of. When I arrived at the Plaza, the sweat was fuckin' drippin' off me! Mammy had fastened the frilly bit to my shirt, ensuring that it wouldn't come undone. I think she even put a few wee stitches in it, to make sure it would *never* come off! It was beginning to feel like a fuckin' *straitjacket!* When Davey saw the state of me he thought I must be running a temperature but thankfully, when I explained my problem, he quickly removed my duffle coat and got me to stand in front of the huge fan that was kept at the back of the stage. As it happens, I soon cooled down and began to appreciate all the effort Mammy had gone to when I saw myself in the mirror. Standing beside some of the band, I didn't look out of place at all!

After the sound check, which included my two numbers with the band, Big Willy explained to all of us the proposed format of the evening. Brian Ferry would be the compere for the talent competition which would take place between 7.30pm and 9pm. Because of the revolving stage, the half that was facing rearwards and out of sight would be set up with the Ferrymen's equipment. The front half, obviously facing the audience, would be set up for the talent competition, with an array of microphones and an organist to assist those in need of accompaniment. At about 9pm the three judges, with Brian Ferry, would retire to his office to decide on the outcome of the competition i.e. first place and the two runners-up. Meanwhile the stage would revolve and the Ferrymen would immediately spring into action with me coming on near the end of their set and finishing at about 9.45pm. The stage would revolve once again with Brian and the judges coming round into view and announcing the results. After the results, anyone on the premises under the age of sixteen would have to leave by 10pm at the latest. Big Willy reiterated the last instruction for my benefit, to ensure that I wouldn't chance my arm and get caught out in the dance hall after that time, putting a future performance of mine with the band in jeopardy! I nodded my understanding of the instructions.

Anyway, at 7.30 sharp Brian came on stage, with the organist belting out a lively wee tune that Brian sang along with. They both then cracked a few jokes but were soon introducing the first of about twelve acts, and I've got to say some were rubbish, some were pretty good, with one duo in particular that were *red fuckin' hot!* About two acts from the end Davey Baker gave me a shout and I made my way to the back of the stage. He asked if I was still up for it, to which I replied, *"Yer fuckin' right I am!"*

Eventually the contestants had all finished their acts, the stage revolved to deafening applause and screams, with the Ferrymen in all their finery, flashing lights, and without doubt a dazzling first set of three rock 'n' roll numbers that had the whole place chomping at the bit! I was seated to the side of the stage just behind the side curtain. There was enough room for me to see what was going on but I was unseen by the audience. I was busy going through the motions with my drumsticks with each number, just like Davey told me to do!

Then at last Big Willy introduced me, and I sauntered on stage as if I'd been doing it for years. My past experience with the pipe band competitions, the Dramatic Society and all the practice with Davey and the show band stood me in good stead. The first number was *'What Do Ya Wanna Make Those Eyes At Me For?'* It was a great tune for a drummer because of the stops and starts, the saxophone players were laying it on pretty thick, and with Big Willy and the rest of the boys cracking out the harmonies in absolute style it made it an experience of a lifetime! The response of the crowd at the end of the number was truly amazing. Cheering, clapping hands, shouting for more with many of them now gathered in a large semi-circle at the edge of the stage! I couldn't see much of the crowd because of the flashing lights and they could just about see me over the top of the drums, which made it all much more special! The second number was *'Rock-a-hula Baby'* and once again the whole place was fuckin' *jumpin'!* When we finished, yet again the response, not just by the audience but by a lot of the staff on duty, was unbelievable. All the boys in the band patted me on the back and I walked off the stage that night feeling not just like a minor celebrity but like a *'fuckin pop star!'*

As I was walking past some tables, a woman of, shall we say *huge stature* called me over to her table, congratulated me on my performance and introduced me to her family and friends sitting with her. They had all come along to support her son, who was not just one of the contestants but would be the indisputable winner of the competition! The show band still had one more number to play so I sat down beside her to wait for the results. At this stage she reached into a very large hand bag and discreetly produced a bottle of vodka that she and certain others at the table had been sharing since they arrived at 7pm! You see, in those days there was no alcohol sold at any of the dance halls in Belfast, just soft drinks, so most people got the females in their company to smuggle some in, usually a half bottle of something, using their very lady-like handbags, but in this case about three or four women had smuggled in varying amounts of alcohol that could be disguised with soft drinks bought at the competition. One of the men at the table offered me a drink of lemonade, which he had to hand in a glass filled to the top with ice. Still sweating after my fine performance, I thanked him very much and took a well-earned slug. The next thing I know, I'm heading for the nearby gents with my eyes watering, my nose running and phlegm tasting like acid coming all the way from the bowels of hell! I managed to reach a sink just in time and the colourless substance that came out of my mouth tasted like the aroma of *jaggy nettles!*

When I returned to the table, the man who offered me the drink told me that I had lifted the wrong glass and in fact had drunk a large mouthful of his drink, which was *poteen!* He then offered me the correct glass to which I gave the sniff test and was pleased to see that this *was* lemonade. I drained the glass in one swallow!

At this point the stage had revolved, with Brian and the judges standing in the centre. He invited all the contestants to join them, formed them into a large semi-circle while Brian and the judges stood to the right-hand side, ready to announce the results. I re-joined the lady of huge stature, whose table was on the right-hand side close to the stage where Brian and the judges had taken up their positions. The results were announced in reverse order, with the duo who I considered to be the best as the winners.

Then all hell was let loose! The lady of huge stature called Brian and the judges a load of *fuckin' cheatin' bastards!* With that she then threw one of the empty bottles that she and the people at her table had been drinking from, with the said missile just missing Brian's head and hitting one of the judges on the shoulder before smashing on the stage floor at the feet of the said lady's son. I realised it was her son *(who was a big lump)* when he jumped off the stage, ran to her with tears running down his face, crying, *"Mammy, Mammy, sure ya won't be takin' me te Bangor for the day, now that I didn't win!"*

This was the signal for another barrage of '*cursin' and swearin*' from his Mammy and her cronies, which in turn led the way for other disgruntled parents and supporters of those who were not mentioned in the results to jump on the bandwagon. There were insults, threats, bottles and glasses thrown in abundance, and then the *bouncers* arrived, about half a dozen or so, and then it really kicked off! By this time Davey had caught my eye and signalled for me to join him backstage from where we and the remainder of the band viewed the ongoing fracas! The sight before our eyes was a cross between Laurel and Hardy, the Keystone Kops and an all-out brawl in the saloon in Dodge City! The RUC had to be called to restore order to the place, which they did in a very short period of time. This was my chance to slip away and head for home. Once outside, I could see the last of those being arrested pleading their cases of innocence, with the lady of huge stature threatening to sue the RUC for police brutality!

As I walked through the streets to my home in Divis Flats, with the drizzling rain just about to turn into another shower, with my hood up and my head held high, I thought to myself, *'Where else in the civilised world would a farce like that take place because of a simple talent competition? Fuckin' Belfast, you are definitely a wee gem!'*

CHAPTER 6

THE WEATHER THAT SUMMER WAS PARTICULARLY GOOD, with many afternoons spent playing football, usually up in the Falls Park, or swimming in the outdoor pool situated in the park grounds; although I've got to say it was considered somewhat of an unnecessary risk to swim in the *coolers*, as the outdoor pool was referred to, due to what you might pick up in the way of bugs in the water or glass on the pool floor! On the occasional days when the weather wasn't so good, the swimming pool at the Falls Baths was the preferred place for entertainment and skulduggery!

On one occasion the Gang of Four decided to spend a few hours there. On a previous visit we encountered the wrath of the new swimming attendant, who was very strict and could easily put the *kibosh* on having a bit of fun; but, not to be put off, we were sure that we would find a way of having a laugh! On arrival we paid for our tickets and joined the queue on the stairs behind three wee dolls. We were all having a bit of banter, with us boys boasting who would be the one to break the ice *(the first one into the swimming pool).*

One of the girls remarked that the new swimming attendant was still as grumpy as ever and some of her friends had decided to give it a miss for a few weeks to see if he would change his tune. She summed him up when she said, *"He's a moanin' oul fuckin' bastard, so 'e is."*

Anyway, the changing room doors opened and it was like the start of the Grand National, with the girls to the left and the boys to the right all rushing to get changed and claim the glory of being the *ice breaker*. I was sliding all over the place because the water on the floor from the previous swimming period had not been mopped up, but we were all in the same boat. Finally the Gang of Four were in their swimming trunks, running down the steps, through the small corridor with shower nozzles along both walls, with freezing water spraying out, to ensure that everyone got the obligatory wash before entering the pool; and would you believe it, the wee dolls were already in the water! We all jumped in, the girls screamin' and shoutin', with us boys splashin' and kickin'and then Misery Hole started to give off. *"You will all be thrown out if you don't behave,"* says he. *"Fuck off,"* says I, just under my breath! We all agreed to quieten down a bit, which gave the Gang of Four the opportunity to chat up the girls. Peter, Brendan and I were getting on really well when Brian decided he needed to go to the toilet. He must have needed to sit down because if it was just a slash he would have done it in the pool. I thought he may have been polite to impress the girls. Little did we realise what he had planned, the *bastard!*

Now, our normal routine on the way to the pool was to pick up a packet of crisps or a bar of chocolate from the local shop to eat on the way home, and sometimes share a bottle of Coke. I can never understand, even to this day, why swimming makes most people hungry! Anyway, Brian made his way back to the changing room, picked up his bar of chocolate, which in this case was a *Picnic* bar, ate half of it, hid the remaining half in his hand and re-joined us in the pool. The next thing I heard was an almighty scream of terror, then another one, then another one! People were jumping out of the pool in complete panic! Then I saw it, a *wee turd!* It was just floating round in circles, minding its own business, not bothering anybody, just bobbing up and down. Misery Hole appeared; his face was a fuckin' picture! He was fannying about like a big fruit and didn't have the slightest inclination of how to resolve the situation. All the swimmers had gathered at the exit end of the pool with gasps and sighs of disbelief, when Brian stepped forward and said that with some toilet tissue, the offending article could be retrieved and disposed of. At this stage Misery Hole looked as if he was about to throw up at the very thought that he would be the one to solve the problem! As if by magic, toilet tissue appeared. Brian took hold of it, carefully edged his way into the water, watched by the unbelieving eyes of the now-freezing swimmers, who would not be deterred under any circumstances from witnessing this unbelievably heroic act. Brian managed, with what appeared to be exceptional skill, to wrap up the brown floater, and ran off to chuck it down the toilet. I followed immediately behind him, suspecting he was up to no good. When we arrived at the changing room Brian unwrapped the brown object, offered me a quick bite of the remainder of his Picnic bar which I duly accepted and the both of us nearly pished ourselves! We returned to the pool, which was now almost empty of swimmers, and told Misery Hole that our task had been completed. He glanced up from his desk, his eyes widening by the millisecond, for he just couldn't comprehend the scene that he was witnessing! Then up it came, the multi coloured yawn. He tried to make it to his rubbish bin at the side of his desk but failed miserably. There was puke everywhere! I turned round and there was Brian licking his fuckin'*fingers!*

Once again, it was back to school after the summer holidays. The Debating Society kicked off, as did the Folk Club and the Dramatic Society. We began preparations for our second production written by J.B. Keane which was entitled '*The Field*'. In later years, this particular play was made into a major film starring Richard Harris and Tom Berenger. When some of my friends and I watched the film, I took great delight in enlightening everyone about the content of the storyline and the fact that I had played a principal role, in the stage version at St Gabriel's.

The Pipe Band had a reasonable year on the competition circuit. We picked up only one prize, which was for Marching and Discipline; however, our comment and score sheets for our musical performance were improving all the time! Coming up to Christmas we were booked to play at various parties and quite a few of our pipers were booked for New Year's Eve celebrations. All in all, the band funds were beginning to flourish.

December of 1967 was highlighted by my fourteenth birthday! Although Christmas and New Year were just around the corner, being fourteen felt sort of smoo-oo-th. I was no longer a sprog teenager and was also about to enter my last year at school! Being in my senior year at school seemed to have more of an attraction from the girls, who were all a lot more developed in mind and body than us mere boys, *and* more uninhibited than I dared or cared to admit! Maybe I got lucky; I never seemed to go through the normal fumbling of inexperienced hands. The girls sometimes liked to help me out a bit, if you know what I mean.

Séamus returned from Birmingham and started work in a wood yard down near Belfast Docks called McCue Dicks. This meant he would be sharing my room but I was glad to see him back in one piece! When he wasn't working he was out playing darts or spending a lot of time with his girlfriend Claire McGurk, who came from Unity Flats and would eventually become his wife. Claire was definitely a wee diamond and looked after me on many occasions in the future, when she and Séamus with their first two children moved to London to set up home and eventually increase their offspring to four.

The early part of 1968 seemed to flash past. With visits down to Dublin with the Gang of Four, St Patrick's Day, and then Easter, followed by a hectic summer term with the Dramatic Society, and the normal high jinks, Mammy made a suggestion that was initiated by Billy. She asked if I would like to go to London for a week or so in the school summer holidays, by boat, and, wait for it, *travel on my own!* I knew being fourteen was definitely the start of something really good! I could hardly believe my ears but jumped at the chance to say a very, very loud *yes!*

Mammy said that she and Billy would sort out the travel arrangements *(travel with someone we all knew, possibly one of Billy's mates on a return trip to London)* but I would have to save very hard and provide my own pocket money. I agreed to everything that was said and you should have seen the Gang of Four and everyone else I told, especially the girls, going green with envy! Some of the comments that were made by the girls were:

"Oh, Brendan, yer goin' te be a man of the world. Yer goin' te be a travellin' man. Oh, Brendan, will ye give us a kiss before ye go?"

I thought to myself, *'I'll give yis more than a fuckin' kiss!'*

Anyway, there was work to be done, and money to be earned, and a hell of a lot of it!

Then one day it hit me right between the eyes! As I was walking up Divis Street one summer evening, the sun was unusually bright with its rays dancing and flashing off the windows in Divis Tower: I thought to myself *'Brendan, me oul son, yer goin' inte the **windy cleanin' business!'***

So, the following day after school, I tasked myself to canvass as many flats as possible in Divis Tower before tea time, to offer the senior citizens an exclusive service with a competitive price with which they would be *highly deeelighted!* Fuck me; easier said than done! The ones that agreed to have their windows cleaned wanted to see the finished product before finances would be discussed! Anyway, onwards and upwards, and so it was agreed by six of the tenants, two from each of the top three floors *(18, 19 and 20),* to begin my trial period on the Monday of the following week, which was the start of the school summer holidays. No problem for an up-and-coming *entrepreneur* like myself! Mammy helped me get my gear together as one of her brothers had been a window cleaner during the war, and she knew everything there was to know about window cleaning, but her expert advice and initial finance would come at a price. Mammy made me an offer I couldn't refuse: to clean the windows in our flat, inside and out once a fortnight for free, *or else!* Mammy nearly heard me swear!

Monday arrived quicker than I had anticipated, and at about ten o'clock that morning I set off in the lift to the twentieth floor, to begin the task of making loads of pocket money for my next trip to London. I had a small stepladder, two buckets, two shammy leathers and a bottle of detergent similar to the one my uncle used during the war. I rapped the letter box at the door of my first customer and was greeted by Mrs Fagan who was about seventy and looked like a typical granny. She welcomed me with a big hello and an even bigger smile. She told me that she was going to the shops and to visit a sick friend but would be back at about twelve o'clock, and if I finished before then to make myself at home until she got back. Anyway, in I went, out she went, and then in went my plan of action. One room at a time, cleaning the insides, followed by the outsides. *Happy fuckin'days!*

The first room was the sitting room, with one large window and with an oblong window at each side going up and down, with catches to prevent them from being opened too wide for fear of something or someone falling out. I had it spotless in no time at all. Then for the outsides; then for the fuckin'*outsides!* In order to clean all of the outside of the large window I would have to get my left arm as far across as possible by stretching through the left-hand oblong window, at the same time holding on to the window ledge with my right hand and balancing myself with both knees on the said window ledge. On looking down from the window, twenty floors up and 200 feet from the ground, I began to have my doubts whether this was going to work or not. There was little chance of me falling out of the small space caused by opening the small oblong window; however, I wasn't sure how much pressure the window catches would take before they snapped! Once half of the large window was cleaned, I repeated the process from the other side and then I realised that the outsides of the two small oblong windows needed to be cleaned as well! After another balancing act with skinned elbows and black and blue forearms, the task in the sitting room was finally completed. I climbed down, stood back and smiled with a great deal of satisfaction at a job, not just well done, but better done than any other fucker could have done!

Using the first window as a template and improving my technique as a contortionist, I was beginning to fly through the rest of the windows like an old pro! By the time Mrs Fagan returned I was having a wee cup of tea and a wee biscuit. To say that she was more than pleased was the understatement of the year! Now it was time for her to pay up, and after a great deal of discussion we agreed that I would accept the princely sum of four bob (20p) *but, but, but*, there was a catch. The crafty oul bitch! She said that since she was my first customer, satisfied though she may be, as a sign of good faith I should on this occasion give her a fifty per cent discount, and she in turn would recommend me to everyone in Divis Tower as an excellent wee worker who gave value for money, and would continue to sing my praises as long as she was charged the same amount on all other occasions! And no one need be the wiser. I thought *'The fuckin' oul bitch has got me by the bollix.'* But hey, what could I do but accept her proposal and swear her to secrecy.

Needless to say I was very wary when I approached my second customer, just in case there was a conspiracy. Thankfully this was not the case and true to her word Mrs Fagan told every man and his dog just how good I really was. At the end of the first day, having completed four flats, even with the oul bitch's discount I had earned myself fourteen bob (70p).

When I arrived home and Mammy saw the state of my arms, she suggested that in future I wear an old pullover to help protect against any war wounds. I realised if I was to clean windows every day two things would happen: I would run out of steam, and would definitely get fed up, so I paced myself and usually did two or three every other day, Monday to Friday, not weekends. Lo and behold, people were coming to our door to book me whenever I was free, not just in Divis Tower but in several of the maisonettes within the Divis Flats complex! The main problem they had was that the man of the house was too big to reach the outsides of the windows properly, or the offspring were too small to do the job without falling out of the window!

McCann Enterprises were on their way with a few casual helpers from the Gang of Four, although I have to say I was the only one who would go above the fourth or fifth floor of Divis Tower, due to the panoramic view available. Hail, rain or shine, the profit will be mine! And so it came to pass that money was amassed, with *yer man McCann* on his way to London, on his first solo trip to the metropolis, for the first two weeks in August!

CHAPTER 7

O N THE NIGHT OF TRAVEL – I think it was a Wednesday because it was cheaper to travel mid-week – a big strappin' man called Bootsey Begley *(Bootsey was his nickname and I don't think anyone except his Mammy knew his proper name)* called at our flat to pick me up, and with a wee tear in Mammy's eye we set off on foot to the docks to board the Heysham boat. Now Bootsey had worked on and off with Billy and Tony in and around London for quite a while and had been home to Belfast for a wedding. On a few other occasions he had stayed at our house in Scotch Street and at our flat in the Divis, and although he was a likable sort of bloke he always had this strange habit when he got up in the morning, after the night before: when he washed his face and hands he always used our Persil washing powder! I don't know why, he just did! I thought to myself that when we went for a quick wash the following morning before leaving the boat for the London train, I would make sure I was in and out of the washroom long before him so as, in the event of him producing his own washing powder, I in turn wouldn't be associated with this slight oddball. With this in mind I couldn't resist asking him why he chose washing powder rather than soap to wash his face and hands with.

No sooner had I finished the question when he put his hand on my shoulder, stopped me dead in my tracks and said, *"Brendan, son, let me ask ye this. Have ye ever wondered how many places a bar of soap has been? Well let me tell ye. From oxters to arses, from fannies to bollix, from mingin' feet to lice-filled hair! And then these fuckin' eejits rub it all over their hands and fuckin' faces, with pubic hair and wee lodgers free of charge! When I'm not at me own sink, washin' powder'll do for me, son!"*

From that day onwards I made sure I had my own bar of soap well-hidden, and on more than one occasion, just for pure badness, regardless of where I might be, if someone upset me I would make sure that the soap in the bathroom/toilet was covered in piss before I left!

Anyway, we soon arrived at the docks and after a short wait we boarded the Heysham boat. With me in tow, Bootsey headed straight for the bar, ordered a pint for himself and, wait for it, a fizzy orange and a packet of Tayto cheese and onion for yours truly! We soon found a table with two spare seats close to the mini-stage, in the anticipation that there may be some sort of entertainment during the early part of the evening's journey. The bar soon filled up with all sorts of shapes and sizes, both male and female, both young and old, and the party atmosphere soon kicked in. At one stage there were that many people in the bar area it took forever for anyone to get to the bar, get served and then plough their way back to their seats or to wherever they happened to be standing; and the fuckin' boat hadn't even set sail yet! But hey, the craic was ninety! After a wee while I convinced Bootsey that a wee glass of shandy wouldn't do me any harm so he reluctantly agreed that on his next visit to the bar he would bring back a shandy for me instead of the dreaded fizzy orange.

On one occasion when he had to go to the gents, a lovely wee woman and her two daughters *(one was fourteen, the other was sixteen, both with short dark shiny hair)* asked if they could join us at our table so as they could be close to the entertainment, which, they were reliably informed, would start soon after we set sail, which would be in about fifteen minutes. Of course I offered them both Bootsey's and my seats, to the response of gracious thank-yous and smiles all round. By the time Bootsey returned I had managed to get two wee, wee stools, supplied by one of the crew who was fortunately transferring them from behind the bar to wherever and was pleased to offload a couple in my direction. Bootsey was a bit miffed at first when he saw the wee, wee stand-in stool that I had provided, but when the two guitar players/singers started up, the wee woman that had joined us began singing along. With this Bootsey saw his chance to impress her and he joined the sing-song as well.

At this stage I was getting on really well with her two daughters, spinning them a yarn that I had left school in the summer and was now on my way to work with my older brothers in London. Why else would I be travelling on my own, drinking, smoking and even offering to buy them a drink? The wee woman had a half bottle in her bag, so soft drinks all round for them, a pint for Bootsey and a pint for meself! *(Bootsey came with me to the bar, just in case I was challenged for being under age.)* But in those days it didn't really matter as long as you had the money and you behaved yourself. I've got to say I really felt like a man of the world with each sip of my drink, which at this stage had progressed to full pints! Fuck the shandies. And the wee woman allowed the elder of her two daughters to sample a wee drop of her illicit vodka and Coke. I thought, hey, boy, you could get lucky here and you away from home on your very first night!

The party was in full swing when a few of the passengers put their names up for a song with the very talented duo supplying the entertainment. After a short break to enable the duo to sort who knew what, what songs would be sung and in what key, the first of the guest singers took to the mini stage: a woman who was introduced as Mary Ellen from Belfast. Holy God, you should have seen the state of her! Although she was probably only about forty years old, she had become an old woman well before her time. She had shoulder-length blonde hair, with a black parting down the middle, a bright sickly-yellow short-sleeved blouse, a black mini-skirt, bright red stiletto-heeled shoes. She had the most magnificent pair of corned beef legs and nicotine all the way up to her fuckin' elbows!

When she started to sing I was expecting the worst but, my God, Mary Ellen couldn't half chant one out! After the second song, even though she got a standing ovation, the duo explained that in order to fit everyone in, they would have to restrict the guest singers to just two songs each. Mary Ellen gave everyone a great big smile, a wave, and then proceeded to fall over her stiletto heels, went head over tits but, thankfully, landed in a position that didn't embarrass her too much, accompanied by another standing ovation, cheers and wolf whistles from the crowd!

As the night progressed most of the singers gave a very good account of themselves with their supporters making comments such as *"Just close yer eyes an yud think yer were listenin' te Jim Reeves"* or *"He cud've bin in Apra, but he didn't want te leave 'es pigeons."*

The drinks were flowing and the party was just getting better and better!

With the wee woman really getting into the party mood, Bootsey was trying to get the wee woman into the party nude! He was fumbling around her top half like an out of work juggler! Meanwhile I was getting on famously with the two daughters, in particular with the sixteen year old! Would this night never end?

At the end of the entertainment last orders were called and would you believe it, two fights kicked off simultaneously, one at each end of the bar. Bootsey edged us all *(he and I carrying our suitcases)* towards the exit doors and into the main passenger lounge. Once we got there and found suitable seats to settle down and continue the conversation, the wee woman left me with the two girls and she and Bootsey went off to find the cabin that she had organised earlier. She was more than just a wee bit tipsy so Bootsey, being the perfect gentleman, volunteered his services to locate the said cabin. When they were away the two girls explained that their uncle on their father's side was a member of the cabin crew and when he was on duty he was able to provide a two-bunk cabin for a bit of cash in hand, with the two girls lying top and tail in one of the bunks. The uncle would in turn supply the normal tea and biscuits in the morning. Job done!

At this stage I asked the younger of the two girls to look after our suitcases while her sister and I went for a wee juke to see if we could find somewhere open to get something to eat. So off we went up several flights of stairs and, would you believe it, we ended up in a secluded area out on deck. Dark but cosy, I think you could have called it, and absolutely ideal for a wee coort! Fuck me! It was like kissin' a fuckin' vacuum cleaner!

She was kissing and tonguing and puffing and panting like we were all going to be dead in the morning! *Halli – Fuckin' – Looya!* When we eventually returned to our seats we arrived a few moments before Bootsey, who told the girls that due to their Mammy being really tired out, she had gone straight to bed and had asked him to make sure that he guided the girls back to their cabin. I said my goodnights and off they went, which left me with a fuckin' big grin on my face!

When Bootsey came back he couldn't wait to tell me of his near miss with the wee woman. It was only because she had too much to drink that he hadn't made the full score!

"Were yis alright when we were away?" says he.

"Sure, we just sat and talked for a wee while," says I.

"What did yis talk about?" says he.

"Well," says I, *"the wee one looked after the suitcases and me and the other one went up the stairs to a wee dark place, and soon discovered what the back of our throats tasted like, among other things. We didn't do too much fuckin' talkin', Bootsey!"*

A wee while later, once the dust had settled, I stretched out on a wooden seat using my suitcase as a pillow and one of my pullovers to rest my weary head on. Séamus had advised me, especially when sailing on the Heysham boat, when getting the head down for the night in the passengers' lounge, to have the handle/snibs side of my suitcase facing into my head and make sure that I divided whatever loose change I had into different pockets, with any paper money stuffed down the inside of my underpants!

He said, *"The thieving bastards would steal the eyes out of yer head and come back for yer fuckin' eyebrows!"*

I carried out his instructions, slept soundly, woke before Bootsey, had a quick wash *(didn't shave at the time)* and off I went to get a wee cup of tea and a wee bun for breakfast. It wasn't long before the whole place began to come to life and I've got to say there were a few sights that were certainly not fuckin' pretty! On my return to Bootsey, he was sitting with his head in his hands as if he was nursing a sore head. When I asked if he was alright he said, *"Me fuckin' wallet's been fuckin' stolen! They even tuck me fuckin fegs! And I've only got a few coppers in fuckin' change!"*

Well, I had to try very, very hard not to laugh, but for fuck's sake, when the water started to form around my eyes, he took one look at me and asked if I was OK. I answered as quickly as possible and told him it must be the beer from the night before that was making my eyes look bloodshot.

Bootsey then said, *"Don't worry, son, when you've travelled as much as me and experienced as much as me, you'll be alright."*

I nearly pished meself, made a quick excuse and ran to the toilet as if I was going to sick! It took quite a while before I got up the courage to go back and face the fuckin' eejit and then he said, *"Can you lend me a few bob 'till we get to London? It's for a wee cup of tea and a packet of fegs!"*

At this stage I really had to take a deep breath, compose myself and, making sure I didn't look him straight in the eye, produce some loose change for the said items! At one stage he thought I was crying and said, *"Don't worry, son, you'll get used to being away from home and standin' on yer own two feet, just like me!"* This was the signal to take my hankie from my duffle coat pocket; and cover me fuckin' face! I was never as glad to get on the London train that morning and pretend I was fuckin' sleepin'!

On arrival in London we were met by Billy at Kings Cross, and after the normal salutations Bootsey headed his way and Billy and I ours. On the Tube to Billy's place I told him about the events of the boat trip over, of course including the part of Bootsey's bad luck. Well, Billy burst out laughing and said, *"Poor oul Bootsey, he doesn't seem to have much luck with the McCanns. The first time he met Tony in a dance hall in Belfast called the JIG, Tony and Bootsey had words and Tony gave him a fuckin' hidin'! And the first time he travels with you he gets fuckin' robbed, probably by the lovely wee woman you were telling me about!"* Well, we had a great laugh all the way across London at poor oul Bootsey's expense.

The following ten days were spent having the time of my life. I'd never had so much freedom and I have to say, more importantly, I'd never had so much trust. Of course I got up to a bit of no good every now and again but, overall, I behaved myself. I came and went but always returned to wherever I was staying at the time and made sure I didn't give any one any unnecessary worries or serious concerns. I was using the Underground like a seasoned traveller, and when I had to use trains going in and out of London, having received detailed instructions from those who must be obeyed, I always got from A to B in one piece and on time! My travels took me from Billy's to Monica's to Gerry's to Frank's (picking up a few bob for extra pocket money along the way) and then to Pat's, who was stationed at Windsor with the Irish Guards. Pat met me at the station early one morning and we made our way to his married quarters in Victoria Barracks, just in time to say hello to Pam and their firstborn, drop off my bag, and walk the short distance to the barrack square to view the form-up of the Windsor Castle Guard. The sight of the bearskins and tunics was unbelievable, especially up close and personal! When the Guard marched off with the Corps of Drums *(flute band),* drum major and their mascot *(an Irish wolfhound called Fionn),* and the wolfhound's handler leading the way, I was amazed at how many people had gathered en route to watch the parade. As we progressed on our way Pat was explaining who was who, what they were responsible for, and what to expect on our arrival at Windsor Castle.

When we got close to our destination, we had to turn a corner to gain entry to the street to the main entrance and that's when I got a full frontal of this magnificent, historic and fairytale castle. I was speechless but was soon brought back down to earth when I realised just how many tourists had turned up! The Micks marched through the main entrance, halted outside the guardroom opposite the old guard *(those coming off duty),* as if they owned the fuckin' place. The changing of the Guard took place with Pat giving me a running commentary all the way through. The Corps of Drums played incidental music while the ceremony took place and what a surprise I fuckin' got. They played good oul foot tapping music, popular music, and lo and behold, they began playing Latin American fuckin' music!

I honestly didn't know that a flute band could play such a variety of music and play it so well! My eyes were certainly opened that particular day, to say the least.

When the ceremony was completed the Old Guard with the Corps of Drums etc. marched back to barracks, with me remaining extremely overawed. Pat then took me for a whirlwind tour of Windsor and lunch in a local pub where, surprisingly, he was well-known.

That night Pat and Pam took me another short distance through barracks to the Sergeants' Mess. Pat had to explain to me what a non-commissioned officer was; fuck me, I didn't know our Pat was some sort of an officer! Anyway, the night started slow with a few people coming and going, then more came than went, then more came and before long there was a real party atmosphere. Pat sorted me out with a few wee shandies and introduced me to just about everyone who was there. I couldn't believe how fast the time went; we didn't leave until about three in the morning! Thankfully we all had a lie-in followed by an enormous cooked breakfast and a few bob for extra pocket money!

Anyway, later that day Pat walked me back to the station with detailed written instructions, for I was to begin my most challenging journey into and around London and then on to meet Tony in a wee pub called the Old Crown in a wee place called Hayes in Middlesex.

Not surprisingly, I arrived in one piece at Hayes and Harlington station. I turned right out of the station, over a wee bridge and the Old Crown was on the right. My instructions from Pat were to go inside the pub. If Tony wasn't there I was to say who I was to the bar staff and they would look after me until such time as Tony would arrive. It was about five o'clock on a Friday afternoon and the pub was already very busy with pints of all sorts of beers and spirits lined up all along the bar, with all the men standing and a few women sitting on stools. Some of these guys were throwing paper money over the bar like fuckin' confetti!

One of Tony's mates called Jimmy spotted me and straightaway he said, *"You must be Tony's brother. He told me to watch out for you and he'll be here pretty soon. Come in and join the party.'"*

With that Jimmy introduced me to just about everyone in the pub and the first pint of shandy appeared, as if by magic. The juke-box was blasting out a load of Irish music, people banging glasses, stamping their feet and joining in with all the choruses, when the door opened and Tony made his grand entrance! He was with about a half dozen mates who I was to discover later were referred to locally as the Crazy Gang! And, by fuck, they were certainly fuckin' crazy! They performed balancing acts, arm wrestling, trick shots on the pool table, drinking feats that defied all logic, glass eating that defied even more logic; oh yes, and there was a very heavy card school going on in the corner, with rolls of money changing hands like they had a licence to print their own! Then the challenge of the decade was made. One of the fairly new guys to the area, who had only been using the pub for a few weeks previously, decided he would like to challenge Tony to a wager. This included the following.

Both of them would have to down a pint each, strip off to their underpants, dive into the canal immediately outside the Crown, and swim along the canal to the next pub *(which was called the Wolf Pack and about 200 yards away);* on arrival at the Wolf Pack, down another pint each, dive back into the canal, swim the return trip, and on arrival back at the Crown, down another pint each. They would put £20 each behind the bar at the Crown, winner takes all *(a lot of money in 1968)!*

Well let me tell you, the place was fuckin' jumpin' with excitement! It was like something out of a John Wayne film except this was for fuckin' real! Tony was strutting up and down the bar like the local champion and the new guy looked like the young pretender. Jimmy, whom I met earlier, 'phoned the Wolf Pack to warn them to get the pints ready then blew the whistle for the start of the race. Tony drank his pint, stripped off and was in the water in a matter of a few seconds, with his adversary, who was a bit slow with the pint but was soon stripped and in the water, not too long behind Tony. The pub emptied into the side street beside the canal, waving and cheering, falling over each other, spilling drinks, shoving and pushing, laughing and staggering with me almost being shoved into the canal!

In the distance it looked like both swimmers were pretty much neck and neck, with the young pretender just maybe edging in front but we couldn't be sure. At last one of them got out of the water and ran into the Wolf Pack to down his pint. The second swimmer, who was some time behind the first, crawled out and struggled to reach the pub and his pint. Within a short period of time the leader dived back into the canal and was propelling himself through the water like a fuckin' torpedo! The next thing I know, Jimmy is calling everyone back into the Crown for a free drink. Needless to say, the stampede nearly took the door off its hinges. As the free drinks were being poured Jimmy asked for everyone's attention and made the following announcement.

He shouted, *"McCann's just been on the 'phone from the Wolf Pack and said yer man can swim like a fuckin' dolphin, drink the 40 quid!"*

A bloody great cheer went up, and when the winner came staggering through the door, another bloody great cheer went up, and when Tony finally came staggering through the door, another bloody great cheer went up. Fuckin' great! Both contestants shook hands, took their underpants off and threw them into the canal and *another* bloody great cheer went up! I looked at my watch and it was only half past six! What next?

A great night was had by all and the following day, which was a Saturday, began with a huge breakfast at the local cafe followed by a tour of Tony's mates' houses and a load of their local pubs and clubs, ending up in the working men's club adjacent to the Catholic church in the town centre. There was a great live band on that night, and although the place was packed there was a great party atmosphere with people of all ages, family groups, all tripping the light fantastic. I knew then that Tony and the Crazy Gang worked hard and played even harder! How in God's name did they do this every weekend?

Sunday morning began at a less frantic rate than the day before as not everyone could face another breakfast, including me. However, after a bit of banter and a bit of slagging, Tony and I met up with a few of his mates in the Crown at about ten o'clock. Bearing in mind the pubs didn't open until twelve o'clock,, there was already about a dozen or so in there, getting it down their necks 'cause they were back to work the following day! I've got to say, at this stage I noticed quite a few of them getting their drinks on the slate as they had literally spent or lost every penny that they had and, I was later to learn, some would have to get a sub from behind the bar to see them through until the next Friday, when the whole thing would start again! Alas, the things a Paddy will do to justify enjoying himself!

On that very hot Sunday afternoon Tony walked me the short distance back to the railway station, made sure I knew the way back to Billy's place, gave me a few bob for extra pocket money, and off I went having had one of those weekends that needed absolutely no enhancement whatsoever to emphasise the downright unbelievable madness of the whole episode!

The last couple of days in London were spent buying souvenirs, catching up on some sensible sightseeing, saying goodbyes and thank yous to family and friends, and just resting up prior to my journey home which, it was decided, I could make perfectly well on my own! And to celebrate my new found individualism, I bought myself a packet of five Manikin cigars! I think Billy cottoned on that I smoked now and again but I kept the cigars well hidden until he left me onto the Heysham boat train, when I sat back in a nice comfortable seat in a smoking compartment and puffed away like the wee wanker I probably looked like!

On arrival at Heysham that Wednesday night, there wasn't the usual stampede to the bar area or to the passengers' lounge due to the fact that most people who were coming back off holiday didn't have much money left, and because it was fairly quiet on that midweek crossing. Ah now, that's where I was lucky because of my sensible business mind and my frugal spirit. Because of all the extra pocket money I had picked up on my travels, I had almost as much pocket money on the way home as I had when I first set out with Bootsey two weeks earlier! Not bad for a wee lad of my age, eh?

I wondered how long that money would have lasted if the Crazy Gang had got wind of it.

Maybe on my next visit to the Crown, I could go into the money-lending business, something I tried later in life for a brief but successful period of time with a great friend of mine from Tipperary, called Kevin Fraser.

Anyway, after getting something to eat and not having the company of an adult, I thought it a good idea to stay away from the bar so, after a wee dander round the boat, I found a comfortable area in a quiet part of the passenger lounge, settled down with my new up-market holdall that Gerry had given me, and proceeded to get bored like any other almost-fifteen-year-old; when, lo and behold, I heard the jingle of coins, the odd banging of a glass, followed by the odd *fuck ye!*

Over in one of the corners of the lounge there were five fellas, aged about nineteen or twenty, playing cards. Now, being a bit of a card player meself, I couldn't resist the temptation to have a wee juke and see what they were up to. There was quite a bit of money on the table to be won, and while I was eavesdropping I discovered that it was due to some good luck that they had on a previous game while on the boat train from London, at the expense of a couple of culchies who were on their first trip home to some obscure place called Bally Slatta Maguttery.

As the night wore on, although they weren't in a heavy drinking session, they were obviously becoming quite free with their ill-gotten gains by placing unnecessarily high bets on some shite cards. One of the players happened to notice me and asked, *"Do ye fancy a wee hand, wee lad?"*

I replied quite simply, *"Aaye, why not?"*

To which one of the others said, *"Sure, 'es only a wee shite who'll cry as soon as 'e loses 'es first fuckin' hand."*

Another of the players then said, *"If u've got any money, put it on the table."*

I placed a good handful of loose change on the table, ensuring that I kept my paper money out of sight, then I just smiled and said, *"If yis still want to play Pont"* (known as Pontoon or 21s) *"that's alright we me."*

This latest comment was greeted with minor cheers and jeers, and then the gambling commenced. Now for those of the unlearned fraternity, let me give you a quick rundown of the dos and don'ts of Pontoon!

Firstly someone is nominated as the banker. On the start of a new game it is normal for the cards to be turned over face up, one at a time, and each card is placed in front of each player in rotation until someone gets the first black jack. That player then becomes the banker. Now, it's the banker's responsibility to cover all individual bets. Each player bets on their own individual cards that are unseen by anyone else and their objective is to achieve a score of 21, or as close as possible without going above that score. If any player goes above that score they are Bust i.e. lose their bets to the banker.

If a player achieves a score of 21 or under using five cards, that is known as a five card trick and can only be beaten by the banker by a lower-scoring five card trick or Pontoon i.e. an ace and a face card or a ten.

If any player is lucky enough to get Pontoon, providing the banker doesn't also get Pontoon, then that player wins his bet and takes over as the banker.

In the event of any individual player's score and the banker's score being the same, then the banker is the winner, so the object of the game is beat the fuckin' banker, or loose yer fuckin' money! Don't worry, on the job training will be provided!

It took me quite some time to orientate myself with the run of play but I began to make some good calls, a wee bit at a time. As I said earlier, I had the good sense to keep my paper money out of sight. However, every now and again one of the other players needed to change a £1 note for loose change to enable them continue to place coins on the cards for their turn to bet, so I made sure I had enough spare coins in front of me so that it was I who made the exchange and in turn placed the note safely in my pocket, ensuring that I didn't have too much money on show in front of me, especially when I was lucky enough to take over the banker's role after I had achieved Pontoon. Then it all started to get a bit hairy!

Time and time again, when some of the players got good hands, I got better hands. When someone got a five card trick, I got a better one. When someone got Pontoon, fuck me, so did I! The back of my shirt was beginning to stick to my back. All the time I was making sure that any paper money I had won was still going into my pocket and remained out of sight.

There then came a welcome break in the proceedings when two of the players needed to go to the toilet, and another two went to the bar for a few more drinks before last orders were called. I cheekily asked for a glass of Coke with ice. Hey, if looks could kill. Meanwhile a well-meaning member of the bar staff who was collecting glasses and emptying ashtrays gave me some sound advice.

Under his breath he said, *"Son, I'll keep this one talkin', an' you pick up yer bag an say yer goin' fer a pish. Go through the wee staff door at the side of the bar an' wait at the other side fer me."*

I tried to explain that I had the situation in hand when he just glared at me and said, *"Right fuckin' ney!"*

I was about to pick up the loose change on the table that belonged to me but another glare from my new-found guardian angel persuaded me otherwise. Off I went, as quick and as quiet as a wee mouse, made my way through the said door and found myself in a wee store room for the spare barrels of beer. Not too long behind me came yer man, laughing his balls off. He explained that had I not followed his advice, I could have well been filled in, had all my pockets emptied, and in turn would have found myself swimming the rest of the way to Belfast!

He showed me through another door and eventually into, wait for it, only the first–fuckin'–class passengers' lounge. He said that I would be safe enough there for the rest of the journey provided I didn't get cocky and start wandering round the boat. I thanked him for his time and trouble, but still I couldn't believe my luck, although he did remark that I reminded him of himself a lot of years and a lot of card games ago.

When we docked the following morning in Belfast, I went to the posh washroom of first class, had a quick splash round me face *(still didn't shave),* and made my way to the gang plank to disembark. I reached inside my duffle coat pocket and produced my last Manikin cigar and lit it up, blew a ring of smoke in the air and swaggered my way off the boat and down toward the dock side. After all, even after leaving behind the wee amount of loose change on the card table the previous night, I was still nearly £8 up! Quite a bit of dosh for someone of my age to be walking around with. Don't forget this was before decimalisation!

Then suddenly I saw them both, Mammy and Paddy. They thought they would surprise me and had come to meet me, to make sure I was okay after making the journey on my own. Holy fuck, I nearly swallowed the fuckin' Manikin cigar! What I did do was inhale a huge and unhealthy amount of cigar smoke. After quickly getting rid of the cigar, I tried to give them a shout and started to cough my guts up.

Mammy and Paddy didn't see me at first because they were at the second-class end of the boat. By this stage I thought I wasn't going to make it home without the help of a fuckin' coffin! Then I saw the five buck eejits from the card school on the previous night, hung over and just about to make their way down the second-class gangplank. Eventually I managed a scream to get Mammy and Paddy's attention but unfortunately, at the same time I managed to get the attention of the first two of the five buck eejits*!*

Mammy took one look at me and said, *"Jesus, son, ye luck an awful colour o' green, so ye do. I knew ye wer too young te travel on that big boat on yer own, so a did."*

With that said, Mammy and Paddy bundled me into a taxi. At the same time, the five buck eejits were yelling at us, waving at the taxi to stop, when Mammy said, *"Were they some friends ye met on the way over, son? Sure, yud bide the time o' day or night with anybody, so ye wud."*

When we arrived at the Divis I had recovered enough from the sickness caused by the cigar, and the fright caused by my gambling colleagues to suggest to Mammy and Paddy that I should pay for the taxi, to which Mammy remarked, *"Ah Jesus, Paddy, sure ye cudn't falt the wee man, so ye cudn't!"*

CHAPTER 8

BACK TO SCHOOL AFTER THE SUMMER HOLIDAYS led into another busy routine. The third play of the Dramatic Society was by Séan O'Casey, called *The Shadow of a Gunman*. Once again the Debating Society and the Folk Club were in full flow and the Pipe Band practices began with a bang, in the guise of two brothers called Charlie and Bobby Rae.

Now, these two guys took their lives in their hands every so often to travel from the location of their band room in south Belfast, situated at the Donegall Road end of Roden Street **(aka *The Village*),** to teach our drum corps in west Belfast in the Lower Falls. They were both natural geniuses! Before long they improved our standard by 200%! I just couldn't believe my eyes and ears, such was the magnificence of both their talents.

At that particular time in the island of Ireland the three top bands were St Patrick's of Donaghmore, Finton Lawler from Dublin, and the Robert Armstrong Memorial from Belfast, with the Rae brothers both playing for the latter. Unfortunately, at the time of writing this, both Rae brothers are no longer with us, and only Finton Lawler remains in situ and actively competing, albeit in Grade Three, not Grade One, but I will be watching their progress with great interest!

Now, I have to make a particular personal point at this stage. The Robert Armstrong Memorial Pipe Band was extremely talented and was without doubt the smartest turned-out band that I have ever seen.

Then and now! With their Dress Stewart kilts, waistcoats, Bonnie Prince Charlie jackets, whiter than white shirts with butterfly collars, black bowties and to top it off, black Tam O'Shanters; and under the direction of their Pipe Major Tommy Geddes they were all absolutely EEEEmaculate! Every last one of them!

Throughout the coming competition season and subsequent seasons I was to learn a great deal more from the Rae brothers, not just about wanting to improve, not just about wanting to win, but how to form a comradeship with my fellow competitors, and as I began to improve in leaps and bounds, to assist less fortunate drummers by passing on the skills that were passed on to me in Belfast. Charlie and Bobby Rae probably never realised just how much of an effect they had on the likes of me and all the others that they took the time to help over a period of many, many years. God bless them both!

My fifteenth birthday was fast approaching when I received some disturbing news! The school-leaving age was fifteen which meant that wherever in the school year that an individual's fifteenth birthday occurred, then that particular individual left school at the end of that term, i.e. summer, Christmas or Easter.

However, the Christmas leaving was cancelled, as was the first step in also cancelling the Easter leaving, which would eventually lead to school-leaving being at the end of the summer term only. This in turn would lead to the school-leaving age being extended to sixteen!

Fuck me! I was getting out just in time but I had to stay on until the following Easter, which really did my fuckin' head in! An extra three months at school when I could be out earning money.

But as they say, every cloud... Due to the fact that I had, over the last year or so, taken part in a number of Dramatic Art festivals, I was fortunate enough to win several diplomas for, wait for it, *Elocution and Dramatic Art*. An offer of a non-paying student vacancy came through from the Lyric Youth Theatre, via the Arts Council, via Pat Brannigan to me. The offer was a one-year scholarship to attend once a week on a Monday night at the Lyric Youth Theatre in Cromwell Road in south Belfast, just off Botanic Avenue. Pat Brannigan advised me most strongly to accept the invitation as it could lead to better things, and possibly if I worked hard, impressed the powers that be, then a second year of scholarship could be on the table! The course was to begin in January, and had I not been included at school in that term and a prominent member of the Dramatic Society then the scholarship might well have been offered to either someone else or, even, to another school. It was explained that the Arts Council were targeting someone who would be able to attend the Lyric Youth Theatre prior to and post leaving school. Pat Brannigan said that it would suit me right down to the ground and I have to say I had to agree. You should have seen the GOB on Mr McGuinness' face (my headmaster) when he was made aware of the news. After embarrassing me to death by announcing my good fortune one morning at school assembly, he came to see me later that day, shook my hand, patted me on the back, and he and Pat Brannigan spoke to me for some time about staying on at school to at least the summer to complete my GCE *O-levels, (as they were in those days)* before deciding to go into the big wild world to earn a living; but I was determined to leave school at Easter, bearing in mind that my mate Brian McAleese had left school the previous summer and was working at Shorts Aircraft Factory.

While all this was going on, Maura and her boyfriend Séamus Doherty set a date for their marriage, which was to be in November at St Peter's Cathedral, and afterwards the reception was to be held at the Orchid Bar/Night Club in King Street near the centre of town.

Mammy and Paddy ordered me my first made-to-measure suit for the occasion and my buddy Brian was also invited. His parents in turn bought him suitable garb and on the day we both looked like two wee spivs!

On the Saturday morning in question, my brother Séamus arrived in good order but slightly hung-over from Friday night's usual high jinks. He was also invited to attend another wedding that day but obviously attended Maura's with a view of flitting from one reception to the other throughout the day, as the distance took only five to ten minutes to walk. Young as I was, even I knew that his plan was, at the very least, foolhardy!

Anyway, Maura turned up and was very much the traditional bride, looking lovely in her white wedding dress, and very, very *late!*

Her intended waited patiently; tall, dark, with his usual sense of very dry humour, and when the best man asked if Maura would definitely turn up he said, *"Well, she said she wud!"*

With the wedding ceremony and photographs completed, off we all went in a convoy of various cars to the Orchid Club. In typical Belfast fashion it didn't take long for the party to get into full swing, and by late afternoon with the entertainment at its height, Brian and I were called to perform on the small stage. We sang a few songs, told a few jokes and presented a comic sketch we had been working on. We both revelled in the applause accompanied by cheers, back-slapping and the odd wee shandy.

My brother Séamus was beginning to show signs of weariness and his journey back and forward through town was becoming more like a long-distance, side-stepping stagger but he managed to make a good account of himself. I began to wonder if he had a wee fancy piece at each wedding party and was waiting for the ok for a bit of rumpy pumpy before committing himself. Either way, by early evening he was hardly fit to chew his fuckin' *fingernails!*

At this stage Mammy was holding court with her wee sherry in her hand when I noticed Paddy coming out of the gents, looking the worse for wear with his right hand covering his mouth. When I asked if he was ok he tried to answer me but his reply came out as a complete garble. Then I realised that his false teeth were missing, *top and bottom!*

We both went back into the gents and, to my horror, Paddy pointed to one of the toilet bowls which was heavily laden with thick vomit, containing the usual carrots and such like with an aroma reminiscent of the bogs on the Heysham boat!

Fuck me, it almost brought tears to my eyes; I didn't know what to do. I managed to persuade him to sit in the next booth so as no one else would see his predicament. I then re-entered the function room, waltzed up to Mammy's table and discreetly informed her of poor oul Paddy's plight, trying very hard not to laugh. She simply excused herself and followed me to the toilets. On arrival she told me to check that it was ok for her to go in, and quick as a flash she was in the gents with me in tow to identify the said toilet bowl. After quickly checking that Paddy was still in one piece, she rolled up both sleeves and vigorously attacked the vomit-ridden shite pot!

Suddenly, I felt the extra bit of icing from the wedding cake I had earlier making its return journey up my windpipe, but due to my reluctance to accommodate its wishes half of it went back whence it came and the other half made its exit down my nose, making my ears pop in the process! I began to feel dizzy but a splash of cold water on my face and a quick drink from the nearby sink helped me to fend off any further nausea. No sooner had I dried my face when Mammy was stood at the other sink scrubbing Paddy's false teeth with a wee scrubbing brush that she had produced out of mid-air! Next it was Paddy's turn, only Mammy was probably a wee bit rough with him for he got a scrub with the same wee scrubbing brush, and with his false teeth back where they belonged, his hair combed, his face washed, he looked and felt like a new man. *Job done!*

Although I've got to say Paddy was complaining about the taste of the beer for the remainder of the party.

"Hey, Madeline, this stout tastes a bit funny. Not funny ha ha, but funny peculiar!"

My fifteenth birthday in December was a bit of an anti-climax due to the fact I wasn't leaving school at Christmas and would begin 1969 as just another schoolboy, not as a wee working man. The festive season came and went with a few paid gigs with the Pipe Band, and in early January I reluctantly made my first school journey of the New Year, but my spirits were lifted when I attended my first class at the Lyric Youth Theatre.

The classes were to begin at 7.00pm and finish at around 9.00pm, depending on the course work being undertaken at the time. I made sure on the first night that I arrived nice and early so as I could have a wee juke round and familiarise myself with the amenities.

I was met by a wee woman of about forty years of age *(ancient in my eyes)* with short ginger hair, dressed in a pair of jeans and an old jumper. Now, wee ginger immediately made me feel at ease explaining that she, in fact, was one of our two tutors and asked me to assist in booking in the remainder of the class as and when they arrived.

I thought to myself, *'Fuck me, I've only just got here and I've got a job already!'*

Within the next half-hour or so everybody who should be there was there and I got to meet them all first hand. I couldn't remember all their names but hey, they all knew mine! There were about twenty-five in all with me being the youngest, a majority being between sixteen and twenty-one with a few a wee bit older; and, wait for

122

it, more than half of them were girls and not a *dog* among them. I thought to myself *'There really is a God.'*

That first night at the Lyric just flew by and before we left for home, there was a scramble for the coming term's programme. Most of us discussed it in as much detail as possible but as wee ginger said, just take it one week at a time. This first class was more of a familiarisation exercise for all concerned and we would all meet the second of our tutors the following week. From there on it would be up to the less experienced members of our class to determine the speed of our progress. If, however, it was a lack of enthusiasm and hard work that delayed our progression, those guilty parties would be shown the door. Wee ginger made it quite plain that slackers would not be tolerated!

At the age of fifteen I felt that I was a bit long in the tooth for the kids dance at the Plaza on Saturday afternoons. The Ferrymen Show Band had moved on to do other things so even a wee jamming session with them was rare. The mainstay of entertainment at a lot of the dance halls was becoming a transition to disco fever and fast becoming more expensive!

I was envious of Brian earning a wage, so in order to earn some extra spending money I decided that a return to window cleaning at the Divis was the best way forward. Every Saturday up until I left school at Easter I would set off at about 10.00am and work through to about 5.00pm, just stopping occasionally for a wee cup of tea and a biscuit or anything else that was on offer. The first few Saturday nights I was too tired to go out but hey, it was worth it in the end. There is definitely something in having a few bob in your pocket. It sort of gives you that extra bit of confidence, especially with the wee dolls.

On one such night I was at a local burger bar in Divis Street when three wee Millies came in. Now, Millies was the nickname for the young girls who worked in the mills in and around Belfast and the Lower Falls had its fair share of both. Without exception they always had a few bob to go out on a Saturday night and there was me still at school at fifteen years of age, so it was imperative that I could hold my own in their company regarding finances. I began a conversation with them which developed into good old chit-chat, with all four of us outside leaning against the burger bar window. Suddenly the heavens opened up and in the melee that ensued to gain shelter inside the premises, the good-looking wee blonde one dropped her burger onto the wet pavement. Aha! Brendan to the rescue!

I offered to buy her a replacement with my hard-earned cash. Her two friends did the old nudge-nudge, wink-wink routine. I quickly obtained a freshly cooked, piping hot burger with some onions to assist me in my procurement of the young lady's attention. Sexual activity could very well be on the menu! The shower of rain disappeared as quickly as it had arrived and off we all went for a stroll across Divis Street, through the gap in the side railings of St Comgall's school and into the school grounds to a secluded area between the trees and the bushes. Then, my piece de resistance: out came my packet of *fegs!* All three girls accepted my offer of a cigarette, and within a short period of time we were sat on the grass in a tight wee circle discussing the latest pop music, films, general small talk, and giving the impression that we were all a lot older and wiser than we really were.

Eventually, I steered the conversation round to a very popular pastime practised in the school grounds. I asked the girls if they fancied a wee lumber *(lumber is Belfast slang for necking).* I hardly got the words out of my mouth when the blonde one took the lead and gave me a French kiss! It was something right out of the movies. I couldn't believe my luck.

The next thing I knew, the other two were changing position to join in the fun.

Fuck me pink! I lay back on the grass and let it all happen, *and then it fuckin' did!*

Blondie lay on top of me with the other two fumbling with my belt. Down came my trousers with just a wee bit of expert help from the two pairs of eager hands and then,

Fuckin' disaster struck! All three of them jumped up and ran like blazes towards the gap in the side railings, leaving me with my trousers round my ankles, my pockets turned inside out with my money and cigarettes gone. I then jumped up with my manhood at the ready and tried to catch them but by the time I fell over my trousers a couple of times and put the stiff and disappointed member away, they were long gone. But hey, my pride may have been dented but I fantasized about those three wee dolls for a long time afterwards.

CHAPTER 9

S LOWLY BUT SURELY, EASTER WAS BEGINNING TO get closer, and the thought of leaving school to become a wee working man had my head full of unbelievable expectations, dreams, and absolute fantasies of potential grown-up activities, with all the time in the world to complete them!

Throughout that last term at school I had several appointments with our careers officer *(I think that's what he was called)*. He was not part of our school teaching staff but was sent in from an outside agency to speak to our school-leavers, of which in this particular term there were about ten of us. All appointments were held in the fourth year common room and lasted no more than about fifteen minutes. He was a pleasant enough sort of man but obviously he thought he was pissing into the wind attempting to forge some sort of career plan with a bunch of kids with absolutely *no* qualifications whatsoever, with most of them not giving a flying fuck anyway!

Because of our seniority as pupils, we were allowed to wear our own clothes rather than school uniform providing they were clean and tidy. In a lot of cases the pupils continued to wear uniform quite simply because the only other acceptable attire they had would be their Sunday best. Of course, as the time for leaving school grew closer various parents would not waste the money on another school uniform so inevitably a lot of them were beginning to grow, or had already grown, out of them to such an extent that it became comical for those poor bastards concerned. Not so in my case.

By this stage I had a reasonable up-to-date wardrobe, most of which I had bought with my own money, enhanced by my older brothers when they were home, and of course by Mammy and Paddy. On my meetings with the careers officer I always made sure that, as well as my usual collar and tie, I wore a pair of cufflinks, so luckily for me he took a wee bit more of an interest in my first rung of the ladder of employment. I had changed my mind quite a few times regarding what I wanted to do but eventually he steered me towards the idea of the possibility of working in a sales environment. He said that with my excellent communication skills and my smart turnout I would be an ideal candidate for an interview with the manager of one of the branches of the most successful multiple tailors in the UK at that time, a company known as John Collier's. Without further ado an interview was arranged in double quick time, to take place in the main Belfast branch in Royal Avenue.

When the big day arrived for my interview, Mammy rekindled her role of mother hen and once again she was trying to tart me up like a wee fruit, but thankfully in this case I put my foot down.

"Mammy," says I, *"will ye leave me alone to get ready? I know what te do an' I know what te say, I'm the one with the diplomas!"* (I nearly said 'fuckin' diplomas' but I thought better of it).

On arrival at the shop I couldn't help but be impressed by the three-storey building before me, and thought this might well be a good avenue to go down. I was greeted by a salesman in a dark smart suit, collar, tie and black shiny shoes, who was kind enough to escort me to the first floor. This was where the manager's/cash office was situated where I was introduced to the manager, Mr Danny Lundy. He immediately made me feel welcome and very much at home. We spoke at length about all sorts of things with Kate the cashier, a long-term employee and confidante of Danny's, joining the conversation and probably providing a buffer zone for Danny and me. At the end of a most enjoyable encounter, for that's what it felt like and not a formal interview, Danny told me that if I was willing to start work immediately after the Easter weekend then he would offer me a position for a three-month probationary period! If I proved to be satisfactory the permanent position of junior salesman would be forthcoming. He advised me to speak to my parents and my careers officer before making any kind of commitment. Fuck me! I was so excited that I ran all the way home, not even worrying about my hair gettin' wrecked!

When I told Mammy, I thought she was going to wet herself, and Paddy kept asking me if I was sure that I was offered a proper job and hadn't made a mistake. With Paddy as a Doubting Thomas I decided to speak to my careers officer at the earliest opportunity just to make sure that it wasn't just schoolboy enthusiasm; thankfully, on our next meeting he assured me that I had in fact got it absolutely right and the job offer was definitely on the table! He also commented that I had impressed Danny that much with my turnout and powers of expression that if he hadn't offered me a job with John Collier's, someone else in the trade would have snapped me up! My only worry was being able to live up to their expectations.

The next thing I did was let everyone at school know that yer man McCann was the only successful school-leaver so far and the only one likely to be successful, not just to get a job but a job wearing a suit and collar and tie.

"Who the fuck does ee think ee is?" was just one variation of the countless comments that were said, supposedly out of earshot. Not to worry, for now I was firmly on my way into the big old world of multiple tailors, with a basic pay of £5 per week plus commission. As the slow passing of time got even slower as Easter approached, I

was ready, willing and sure that I would be up to the task when the big day arrived. In the meantime I kept up with my window cleaning, our latest production at the Dramatic Society, the Folk Club and of course band practice and still time seemed to stand still! My mate Brian sympathised with me. He assured me my big day would soon be on the doorstep; and then it was. It arrived with a bang.

My first day at work was to be on Easter Thursday, while all my schoolmates and mates from the Divis were either still on Easter holidays or had conveniently not found a job. I found it extremely difficult to get up with all my mates still in bed, because at eight o' clock in the morning that's where they would all fuckin' be! Jammy bastards!

Mammy had to call me more than just once or twice. *"Jesus, Mary and Joseph, will ye get out of yer bloody bed,"* was just one of Mammy's useful phrases. I finally got up, washed, got suited and booted and was soon on my way, leaving Mammy standing at the front door with a wee tear in her eye as I went off to face the music as I knew I was going to be a wee bit late, on my very first morning at John Colliers: about one hour late to be precise!

When I arrived I made my way to the first floor to present myself to Danny Lundy who on seeing me with a smile on my face asked why I had reason to look so happy. I answered, *"Mr Lundy, here I am, at a quarter to ten, just like you said, but I'm a couple of minutes early.'"*

To which he replied, *"I'm sure I told you to be in at a quarter to nine for opening at nine."* To which I replied, *"Yes, you did at first, but then you changed your mind and said a quarter to ten. Me Mammy thought it was because it was me first day at work after the Easter weekend that you thought to give me a later start, with it being me first day an' all."*

Danny Lundy thought for a moment and then said that he probably did change the time, hesitated, scratched his chin a few times then shouted for Tommy Suitor *(No joking, Suitor was his real name)*. Tommy was about nineteen, had been in the trade for about three years, two of which at John Collier's, and I was to be his understudy. As we walked away from the area of the cash office I could see Kate the cashier through the glass partition give me a knowing smile and a wee wink. I can assure you I was never late for work at John Collier's again!

That Thursday and Friday were very long days, what with being on me feet for such a long time throughout the working day and learning not to slouch but to also remain comfortable when doing so. Little did I know how beneficial these disciplines would be to me, especially when I changed to my future chosen profession. Each night I was in bed early and by the time Saturday morning came, I was having the same problem that occurred on the previous Thursday.

Fuck me! Day three and I was ready to throw the towel in, *aah but* it was Mammy to the rescue for she told me it was a half hour later than it really was and I was up and out the door, and would you believe it, I was ten minutes fuckin' early!

Saturday was to prove even longer and harder than the previous two days. I was rushed off me feet from opening to closing, running up and down stairs, sorting out change, learning how to wrap up the sold items properly; mostly suits so that they would look good when the customer got them home and not with loads of creases that made them look like an accordion!

There was a lift, of course, but with the shop being so busy I didn't have time to hang around to wait for it. Sometimes those using it would not close the two sets of sliding doors properly *(the outer door was solid with a small window and the inner door was a cage-like effect).*

Consequently, being the most junior of juniors it was my job to locate which floor the bloody thing was stuck on, race up or down the stairs, correct the problem, and render the lift active once again; until the next time! It took me quite some time before I realised that the shop staff were, in most cases, the guilty parties. After some considerable thought, it dawned on me that my work colleagues were taking the fuckin' piss! They were adjusting the doors on purpose as some sort of initiation exercise. *The fuckin' bastards!*

I always prided myself on having a great sense of humour but it was certainly put to the test on that first Saturday.

Anyway, six o'clock came at last; the front doors were locked with me on standby with the keys to allow the last few remaining customers to leave once they had finished their business. At about half past six the last slow-coaches of customers and all the staff had gone, except Danny Lundy, Kate and *me!*

Because I was the junior person in the whole shop, it was my job to stay behind with Danny and Kate to be at the disposal of the said two for various wee jobs around the three floors of the shop; i.e. on this first occasion Danny took me through the confirmatory check of the locking up, starting on the top floor where the tailor and staff of the alteration department were situated; down to the second and first floors; and eventually to meet Danny and Kate at the front doors. On the way I was tasked with any last-minute tidying up that may have been missed by the remainder of the staff. Danny did the locking up on all the other days by himself but insisted that a member of staff double-check it on a Saturday, quite simply because the shop would be closed through Sunday until Monday morning so particular attention had to be paid on every Saturday night. I suspected that Danny was using this in my case as an integrity-proving exercise.

My six o'clock finish didn't arrive until just after seven. I was fuckin' knackered! When I got home I had me tea, and had a soak in the bath where I promptly fell asleep.

I woke up to the sound of Mammy banging the door, almost drowning and shivering like a fish out of water, and to crown it all off I slipped and banged me fuckin' head off the fuckin' basterdin' fuckin' door handle. When I eventually opened the door Mammy started petting me like a fuckin' five year old!

After a wee while I calmed down, and sat on the settee to watch TV, nursing an awful sore forehead and asking myself what I had done wrong to deserve the misfortunes of the last three days. It wasn't long before I was snoring my head off and decided to go to bed, at nine o'clock on a Saturday night!

The following morning which was Sunday, Mammy woke me at eight o'clock for nine o'clock Mass, then woke me for ten o'clock Mass, then eleven o'clock Mass! I thought to myself *'Which part of "I'm not fuckin' interested" does **she** not under–fuckin'–stand?'*

But being the God-fearing wee soul that I was, Mammy convinced me that not going to twelve o'clock Mass was not an option! I nearly fell asleep after the first hymn but the next door neighbour, who was a wee oul woman of about eighty, kept nudging me with an elbow that would not have been out of place in the Irish Rugby Team! Was there no end to this torment?

Home after Mass and the usual great big feed of a Sunday dinner was on the table. As soon as I ate that I dozed off again, and continued to doze on and off until it was time for me tea and then I went back to bed! The next thing I know it's Monday fuckin' morning and I've got to do it all over again this week, next week and every fuckin' week! Why oh why did I wish for my school leaving to come so quickly?

Anyway, days turned into weeks, weeks turned into months and slowly but surely I began to make great progress in the art of selling menswear. My commission was also beginning to increase whether I sold sports jackets and slacks, bespoke or readymade suits, rain macs or overcoats, shirts and ties, and even the more expensive Millium lining that could be sold for the back of waistcoats or the inside of jackets for bespoke, two- or three-piece suits, rather than the run-of-the-mill lining provided at no extra cost!

I also developed the technique of sensing when a practical joke was on the horizon. I began to play the game, and soon became a master of turning the tables to such an extent that I welcomed any jovial challenge, wisecrack, nonsensical task at everyone else's peril. It was all a part of the learning curve, growing up fast or getting left well behind at the starting blocks!

My work colleagues became great friends and great allies, with Danny Lundy steering us all in the right direction and Kate always there to give advice, good or bad, to anyone who needed a shoulder to lean on *(several of the senior salesmen dearly wished they could lean on more than just her shoulder!)*.

John Collier's staff came from every conceivable area in and around Belfast as was the case of all the retail shops in the centre of town, so to say my many acquaintances and pals, male and female, were a pretty mixed bunch was certainly an understatement. It led to great nights out after work, especially on Saturday nights, and at the end of the night we all made our own way home, some in the same direction, some on their own, but would all meet up again for some high jinks whenever we could afford it.

I could think of worse jobs and worse people to share the beginning of my working life. What began as an unwelcome chore became a most welcome delight (well, most of the time).

At this stage I had left behind the Folk Club, the Debating Society and the Dramatic Society, although I made frequent visits to Pat

Brannigan to assist with his current production and keep him up to date with my job, but more importantly with my progress with the Lyric Youth Theatre. My mate Brian and I always had our times together and on occasions his brother Peter and Brendan Baxter would join us for a Gang of Four night out. On those particular trysts we were back to our old ways: up to no good and plenty of laughs!

The Pipe Band was improving all the time with competitions on Saturdays or Sundays throughout the summer. We were picking up a few more prizes and a few more gigs. Some of the private parties we played at were being held at various locations in Belfast and some-times on the outskirts of town and, of course, were quite well paid.

Throughout the next two years we travelled all over Ireland with competitions, gigs and parades, including all six counties in N. Ireland, numerous locations in the Republic of Ireland including Donegal, Dundalk, Drogheda, Dublin, and Wexford, and on one trip we travelled all the way to Cork *(They didn't half talk funny in Cork!)*.

Now and again I would play drums for a wee Céilí Band in and around the Lower Falls area. They didn't have a name as such; they just showed up with as many of their fellow musicians as possible, no mikes, no speakers, just plain old-fashioned singing and playing around the table with a few quid and a few pints for providing the entertainment. On occasions I would also be asked to sing a ballad or two, which kept me upfront with any of the other personalities who would have been present that night.

Then one day we were asked to play at an afternoon session. It was to be a Sunday, starting at about two o'clock in the local wee club where a private get-together had been organised to commemorate the passing of a prominent committee member and selector of the local Gaelic Junior Football Team.

The Céilí Band arrived with me in tow at about half past one and immediately set about having a quick drink before discussing the programme for the afternoon. Now, all the pubs at that time were closed on Sundays, which made getting a wee sly gargle on the day of rest almost a mortal sin!

As it was an unlicenced establishment, all the booze had been smuggled in the night before, and a well-presented bar area was at one end of the room, with the Céilí Band area at the other end *(wise decision!)*. The contraband booze was very much cheaper than the normal pub prices, but because of the shortage of glasses, bottled beer was drunk by the neck, and spirits in paper cups *(VIPs, only, had glasses)*.

Anyway, at about half past two the small room was packed with everyone and anyone when one of the organisers *(a VIP?)* banged a table with an ashtray to call all present to order. He spoke for about ten minutes about the late Mr Stevie Walsh, who had spent many a year involved in the GAA *(Gaelic Athletic Association)*. At the end of his address everyone drank to the memory of the deceased, followed by three loud cheers.

That was the signal for the music to begin and begin it did; with a fuckin' Big Bang!

A huge brick came flying through the window and hit some fella on the back of the head, with the glass shattering all over the place.

Quick as a flash, three or four of the VIPs *(they were the ones with glasses)* ran outside to confront the guilty culprits. As I looked out of the broken window I witnessed an all-out set-to between about five or six men who were literally kicking and punching the fuck out of each other! Then they started fighting dirty: someone got kicked in the balls then I heard the sound of *fut* against a nose. Fuck me pink, what a mess that man's face was in. I thought to myself *'Fuck me, this is better than the punch-up in the Plaza dance hall I experienced at the talent competition!'*

It didn't take long for those gathered inside to filter outside to get a better view, and of course word had spread around the neighbourhood, resulting in a large crowd gathering to see the free show. Fuckin' great!

In the meantime the Céilí Band were helping themselves to whatever they could get their hands on to drink *(me included)*, at one stage bypassing the paper cups and swigging from the most inviting whiskey bottles that the good Lord had been so kind to make easily available! We also helped ourselves to a few bottles of beer just in case we got thirsty later. After about twenty minutes some of those with a bit of sense intervened, and managed to put a stop to the disturbance and restore some sanity to the situation.

Wee women from up and down the street appeared with damp towels to help stem the blood from the walking wounded and offer assistance to those involved. Eventually, everyone shook hands and all of the gladiators made their way inside the wee club room, upon which a small speech was made *(by a VIP)* to apologize for the break in proceedings and any inconvenience caused by the unfortunate fracas, and since no one was seriously hurt, there would be no cause for alarm. Once again, there were three loud cheers.

We played our music for about an hour, and I've got to say I've never heard that wee Céilí Band play as well before, so early in the programme. Maybe it was because it was a Sunday?

When we had our break for a well-earned drink *(HEE HEE)*, I managed to find out why the fight had occurred in the first place. Apparently, the man who had thrown the brick through the window was the father of one of the local Gaelic footballers, who was part of the team that the deceased was responsible for. The wee player in question was dropped from the team for no rhyme or reason towards

136

the end of that season, and the father in question didn't agree to an official farewell to the man responsible.

It also transpired that the father in question and the deceased's wife had been having a bit of the other on the side for years! Knowledge of this had become a general point of gossip in recent weeks, in just about every corner of the district.

The window-breaker's answer to that was *"You shud never let yer personal feelin's get in way of the team selection!"*

CHAPTER 10

THROUGHOUT THE SUMMER OF THAT YEAR *(1969)* the tension during the marching season was extremely high; much higher than I had ever experienced before. Although the Gang of Four had our usual get together on the twelfth of July to watch the parade in the centre of town, I thought it wise to stand on the west side of Royal Avenue *(route to Divis Street)*.

This would give us an easy getaway from the parade, up Castle Street and soon after arrive at the Divis, just in case something unexpected kicked off. Thankfully the parade went off without a hitch and the entertainment from start to finish was first class; however, we didn't stay for the return journey of the bands, of which there were many, due to the fact that the gut feeling I had was not to tempt providence.

August that year arrived with a Bang; quite a lot of Bangs if I was being honest.

Riots, gunfire, hand-to hand-fighting, severe injuries.

Deaths, upon deaths, upon deaths!

Burning cars, burning buses, burning houses, burning people!

Deaths, upon deaths, upon deaths!

I remember looking down from our flat in Divis Tower, from the eleventh floor, at the ant-sized people running up and down Divis Street, Dover Street and the Lower Falls.

Screams of agony, screams of horror, screams of delight!

Deaths, upon deaths, upon deaths!

Each night after work was becoming a complete nightmare. Even though our flat was just over halfway up the twenty floors of Divis Tower we still found the need to turn the TV and the lights off at certain times. We also found ourselves crawling around the flat on our hands and knees, such was the ferocity of the situation!

Even when the fighting died down for the night I found it sometimes impossible to sleep.

After only a few short weeks of continuous conflict I was beginning to wonder when it would end and we could get back to normal. Little did I know how naive that thought actually was.

When September arrived I was as pleased as punch because I was going on holiday with the Gang of Four and Mr and Mrs McAleese. We were heading down to Co. Kerry for the Rose of Tralee Festival! We would travel in two cars *(Brian had now got his licence and a car),* with three of us in Brian's car and one of us with Brian's parents. It was agreed that one of us boys would swop over every so often to travel with Brian's parents, with the exception of my good self because in the event of becoming separated I was the most dependable navigator *(good one, says I).*

Anyway, the big day came, the two cars arrived at Divis Tower, I said my bye-byes to Mammy and Paddy, and with the weather much better than normal we began our long journey south, and I've got to say I wasn't sorry to leave Belfast behind.

We stopped along the way, more often as not for Brian's sake as his Mum and Dad were a bit worried that prolonged driving for Brian, so soon after passing his test, would in fact be extremely testing.

We had also prearranged to stop overnight in Dublin; the Gang of Four at my brother Robert and his wife Anne's house, with Brian's parents at a bed and breakfast owned by Anne's auntie.

When both cars arrived outside the house Anne welcomed us all with a great big hug, and proceeded to lay on a lovely spread of tea, buns, biscuits and a huge cream cake! We all tucked in and with the help of my nephew and nieces it wasn't long before most of the goodies were gone.

Robert and Anne were very concerned about the present troubles in Northern Ireland and after quizzing us all in detail, hoped that it wouldn't be too long in sorting itself out. It was soon agreed that an early night for us travellers would be most beneficial, with a bright and early start the following day, for the second and most demanding part of our journey. Up in the morning with a great big breakfast and fond farewells, we were soon on the road. The sun was shining, with not a cloud in the sky; and with not a care in the world, smiles on our faces and singing our heads off, we could hardly wait to get to Brian's auntie's house in Tralee. By late afternoon we arrived at our destination with Brian a wee bit worse for wear. I've got to say, he did really well with all that driving with very little experience. But he soon cheered up when his auntie announced that the circus was in town and a special low-cost rate was on offer for that first night of the show.

We tried to dump our bags in our bedroom – a double bed for Brian and Peter, and bunk beds for Brendan Baxter and me – but Brian's mum had other ideas. Firstly, we had to unpack and put underwear in drawers; secondly, hang up everything else in the wardrobe; thirdly, place our shoes neatly in the bottom of the wardrobe or underneath our beds; and, last but not least, put our washing kit neatly on top of the tall boy *(chest of drawers)*. Fuck me, who invited Adolf?

Anyway, after being forced to eat sandwiches and fruit, the Gang of Four were turned loose on the unsuspecting public of the lovely wee town of Tralee. That first night was fantastic! It was the first time for me to see a proper circus in a huge marquee. In Belfast I had been to theatre shows with sort-of makeshift circus acts that weren't all that good but hey, in this show there were proper clowns that were actually funny, trapeze artists, tightrope walkers, cars that exploded, horses, sealions, big dogs, wee dogs, even wee-er dogs, wild lions and elephants!

The closest I had ever come to this before was the elephant up at Belle Vue Zoo. He was older than the hills, had a limp, and his party trick was eating newspapers and farting like a machine-gun! But this time, I saw the real thing; it was fuckin' great!

At the end of the show one of the locals, who recognised Brian and Peter from previous holidays, told us about the Fun Fair! I just couldn't believe that this night could get any better so off we all went to investigate. Our Gang of Four was now about seven- or eight-strong and we were all hell-bent on having a good time.

The first stop at the Fair had to be the dodgems. There was the usual mad rush to get a car, but Brian and I were successful on our first attempt along with Peter and Brendan, leaving the local hoods standing at the side, just slightly embarrassed. The secret was that all four of us ran for four different cars; that way we nearly always picked up two. We simply shared a car between two, taking turns at driving; piece of cake. These fuckin' culchies hadn't a fuckin' clue.

There were the usual groups of girls on the dodgems, and our two E-Type cars were doing spin wheels, bumping and banging, with the screams of delight from the girls concerned giving us the premonition that they could well be up for a wee lumber *(remember that night in the grounds of St Comgall's School).*

Call it what you like, but all four of us knew that these local girls would give their right arms for a wee bit of city boy banter. After all, we were men of the world, we had a car, we had a few bob, we had up-to-date stylish clothes and we were all working. How do you like those fuckin' apples?

No sooner had we introduced ourselves when we were all heading for the Ghost Train. We decided to pair off with four in each car and off we went into the black hole of Calcutta! The wee dark-haired girl that was paired off with me was clinging on to my arm for dear life, not that I minded. I looked round to see the other three in a similar situation with the local hoods lurking nearby, all standing with faces like thunder. Ah well, in for a penny, in for a pound! Bring it on.

After spending more money that night than we had planned, we walked the girls home. They all lived pretty much in the same part of town, give or take a small street or two. The Gang of Four made sure that one of us kept watching behind, just in case a few of the locals were still pissed off with us for waltzing off with the local totty! Anyway, after the normal moans and groans of adolescent pleasure we boys headed back to Brian's auntie's house and arrived just in time for homemade hot bread rolls, to be dipped into homemade hot soup. Ahhh... sheer bliss. We were all in bed soon after, but not before comparing notes about the goodnight episodes we had with the girls. Peter was in love. Fuck me! What a dick!

The following day we were once again up bright and early, ate breakfast and spent most of the day at the beach at Ballybunion. In fact, every day was a complete gas: pony trekking in the Gap of Kerry, boating on the Lakes of Killarney, watching the street buskers who were on almost every corner or at the front door of every pub, and of course, each night watching the various heats of the Rose of Tralee Festival under the all-weather cover of the open air stage at the main entrance of the town hall, including all its added variety of entertainment from places far and wide. Fuckin' great!

Towards the end of the week our funds were becoming extremely depleted but the cavalry arrived in the shape of Brian's Mum and Dad. They gave the four of us a £1 note each! That, my friends, was a lot of money for a working man and woman to part with in 1969, especially to a sixteen- and three fifteen-year-olds!

With the holiday sadly over we said our farewells to all the neighbours, Brian's auntie, our holiday sweethearts; even the local lads had forgiven us for taking that step too far! We made our way home, once again via an overnight stay in Dublin and eventually arrived in Belfast pretty much completely knackered *(Peter was still in love)!*

Ah well, it was back to the grindstone, and once again, it was my plan to work hard, earn loads of commission and build my finances up for Christmas. However, this was to prove much more difficult than I could ever have imagined.

The troubles had really kicked off as if there was no return. The British Army was now well and truly installed, with uniformed soldiers a common sight in and around the Divis and of course, further afield.

CS gas was a regular feature in the air; particularly in the early evening when I was heading home from work. It didn't take long to suss out that a large gent's hanky was a valuable asset to be carried by anyone with the least bit of sense.

When the CS gas was in the air I would knock on someone's door and ask if I could soak my hanky in some water; the hanky would then be held over my nose, mouth and eyes, peeping around the wet shield to seek my route home, sometimes diverted the long way round due to the breakdown of law and order. It was a never-ending fuckin' nightmare!

Sound sleep was a thing of the past; I didn't even need the sound of the alarm clock to get up for work! Mammy was very taken aback when she discovered that I was up most mornings before her!

With every passing day there would be more shootings, more bombings, more injuries, more deaths, all reported either on the radio, the TV, or in the newspapers, but on some occasions everything was happening so quickly that word of mouth was the fastest way of communicating the latest episode in this perennial cabaret of hate and violence which had finally degenerated into total carnage!!! Had we gone that far that there was no way back? Apocalypse personified!!!

My sixteenth birthday, Christmas and New Year passed without the usual high jinks and celebrations. Travelling around Belfast was becoming extremely hazardous and it was thought very unwise to attempt to travel outside the local area. Since the troubles began in the previous August, business in every line of work had been seriously affected to the detriment of all concerned, including workers, management and business owners. No one escaped the financial burdens of being in the middle of an inevitable industrial collapse!

Thankfully, the Céilí Band and the Pipe Band kept me from losing my sanity! In the early part of 1970 the Rea brothers, due to the impossible situation we all found ourselves in regarding freedom of movement around Belfast, found it difficult to get across to our band room to assist at band practice. They tried on many occasions to reach us by car but the whole situation was just far too dodgy! It was agreed to wait until the competition season began and we would meet up early on the contest days to continue our tuition.

It was also very difficult for the Gang of Four to meet up, although Brian and I quite often took a chance and met up in the centre of town or at the Dramatic Society, to catch up with Pat Brannigan and his latest production. Some of our journeys home were to prove hair-raising, to say the least! Both our parents were very much against the amount of time we sometimes had to spend solo and on foot to get from A to B. But, onwards and upwards and fuck everybody else!

My scholarship at the Lyric Youth Theatre took a dive for a wee while, but eventually the two tutors and almost all of the students once again became regular attendees. It was another most welcome diversion from the never-ending melee of what can only be described as The Belfast War Zone!

A few of the Drama students were also students at Queen's University, and on one particular Monday night when our Drama class had finished, about seven or eight of us made our way to the students union club/bar to discuss our course and to have a bit of craic.

Now, I have to say I was really chuffed to be invited along because I was the youngest by far and was quite impressed by the reaction I got when I accepted. I mean, apart from me, everyone in our company was seventeen, eighteen or nineteen and there were three good-looking girls included who I wouldn't have minded swopping spit with *(and me only sixteen!)* Also, I was the only one who didn't live in a semi or a detached house so at first I thought I should watch my Ps and Qs. However, I needn't have worried because as soon as we arrived I was put immediately at ease with the friendly atmosphere from all concerned.

After a great night, it was well past eleven when we said our goodbyes and time for me to make my way home along a route that would not be particularly favourable for any one in their right mind, regardless of whichever side of the fence they came from. But a promise from the girls that the same gathering would be on the cards the following week put a spring in my step and I got home in double-quick time! Now, the invitation the following week was not just to the club/bar but to attend the open mike night at the folk club, which was being regenerated after many previous members had left due to graduation in the recent past.

Well, well, well. I was sure that, given the opportunity, I would get a chance to impress the organisers and, of course, the girls who invited me. A bit of practice was definitely on the agenda along with several other innuendoes. You can't keep a good man down, *eh?*

The following Monday couldn't come fast enough and before long I was back at Drama class making sure I made an impression, not just with the tutor, but with the crowd that would undoubtedly be going to Queen's later that night.

After a few wee pats on the back from the tutor for my various interpretations of scenes and scripts, the Queen's group also congratulated me on being a team player and offering my personal ideas to be shared in open forum, which of course included the three good-looking girls! No flies on me, *eh?*

Anyway, it wasn't long before the Queen's group made its way to the student's union and into the club/bar. Now, the folk club gathered in a wee room at the back of the club/bar, in order not to annoy anyone else who was there for other reasons i.e. just gettin' full!

There was a small makeshift stage with three mikes and two speakers, with an old record player supplying some background music. There was a good feel about the place, especially when one of the girls in our group put a pint of lager down on the table in front of me. I wouldn't have minded if she put something else down in front of me but hey, I thought, one thing at a time.

On our previous visit to Queen's we had split into two groups so as not to incur too much expense when it was someone's turn to buy a round, and by the looks of things that night the three girls had opted for me to be in their group. Halfway down my first pint the show began with some of the old and bold leading the way, endeavouring to demonstrate how it should be done. To be quite honest, some were quite good while others were not so good. The organizer and MC for the night was a handy guitar player and also a good oul chanter, but he was so far up his own arse, I could understand why some of the potentials in the audience were reluctant to step up and be counted.

The MC seemed to me to be a lot older than anyone else in the room, in fact older than any other student I had ever come across. To be honest, he was at least thirty: fuckin' ancient!

I was reliably informed that he was a mature student, whatever the fuck that was! And he was a Divinity student, whatever the fuck *that* was!

He was quite tall with dark curly hair, wearing jeans and a tweed sports jacket that had threads hanging from every angle and a shirt that was opened halfway down to his waist. In later years I would refer to anyone else dressed in the same way as *Medallion Man!*

Anyway, almost straight away I could see that a percussion instrument would be of great advantage as most of the performers were solo, with a guitar or banjo, or in some cases *a cappella*. On making a brief enquiry to one of the MC's lackeys, I was taken behind the small stage to a small store room where I discovered an array of different time keepers, most of which were damaged or covered in dust and shite! With the help of an old cloth I dusted and cleaned two of the potential showstoppers and appeared with a tambourine and a set of bongo drums. Then, to the smiles and nods of the three girls I put my name down to accompany anyone who found the need for a bit of back-up. Believe it or not, *Medallion Man* was the first to avail himself of my untried talent. He gave the impression that he would use me as a scapegoat to further his own high esteem. What a fuckin' shock he was in for!

He began playing a song called '*Where have all the flowers gone*'. It was an easy song to follow on the bongo drums and, would you believe it, I also knew all the words. I began to offer a wee bit of harmony to the song and at one stage took over as the lead singer, ending in a big finish with *Medallion Man* feeling slightly upstaged. This threw the doors open for everyone else who was feeling a bit apprehensive, and the next thing I knew I was being asked to stay on stage and perform with all and sundry! The three girls at my table were so impressed that no sooner had I finished a drink when another one was promptly placed in front of me.

It wasn't long before a bespectacled spotty female got up with a big fancy guitar and announced that although she was a competent instrumentalist, she was a crap singer. *Aha!* Brendan to the rescue! After a short period of collusion we agreed on a short format of songs to be played in a miscellany *(short versions of two or more songs)*. Apart from a few very minor mistakes that were only to be expected for a first-time performance, we went down like a house on fire. I'm afraid at this stage *Medallion Man* was definitely having a sense of humour failure. This resulted in a short break in proceedings being called by *He Who Must Be Obeyed!* The dopey bollix!

I returned to my table and the waiting girls, who in their wisdom had once again supplied me with yet another drink, but there were also a number of drinks arriving at our table from various people around the room, resulting in me sharing them out with the girls and also saving me money in not having to pay for a round. Fuckin' great!

At this stage I noticed two wee suntanned crackers wearing very tight black T-shirts, black miniskirts and FMBs *(fuck-me boots!)*.

They were each carrying a guitar and asked *Medallion Man* if he could tune their instruments for them. The fuckin' jammy bastard!

Anyway, he steered both girls into the small storeroom at the back of the stage and after giving a furtive look over his shoulder, he firmly shut the door.

A few minutes later another rather older student entered the folk club. She had short ginger hair, and was wearing a white polo neck top, white trousers and white boots. She looked like a walking *Swan Vestas!*

She inquired as to the whereabouts of Maurice. One of the girls at my table told me that Maurice was the MC, aka to me as none other than *Medallion Man*. I walked over to the lady in question and said, *"Maurice is in the back room, tunin' in a coupla G-strings."*

I guided Ginger towards the storeroom and hovered a safe distance just behind her. As she opened the door I positioned myself so as I could see through the gap of the door caused by the hinges. I thought my eyeballs were going to pop out of my fuckin' head!

Both mini skirted girls were in a state of semi undress *(tits out!)*

Maurice appeared to have his trousers down below his hips, with both of the girls giving him the hands-on treatment, all three completely oblivious of the newly-arrived spectator. Ginger screamed, *"Maurice! You dirty rotten filthy bastard!"* All three looked in the direction of the door simultaneously, all three jaws dropped open, and the two girls let go of Maurice's cock as if it was on fire *(it probably was, hee hee)*. Both sets of tits were quickly put back inside their T-shirts, then both girls ran quickly past Ginger and out of the building, possibly even out of Belfast for all I knew!

Ginger gave Maurice such an awful fuckin' dig in the bake! This resulted in a nosebleed. Talk about laugh, I nearly had convulsions! Ginger then did an about-turn and stormed out of the storeroom, screaming obscenities as she, in turn, left the building. Maurice made an attempt to chase after her, offering some sort of pathetic half-hearted excuse of a misunderstanding. At the same time, with nothing else at hand except the dirty old cloth I had used earlier to clean the tambourine and the bongos, he tried to stem the flow of blood spurting from his nose, and with his other hand trying to pull up his trousers and put his well-tuned organ away. As Maurice rushed past me, still pulling up his trousers, I couldn't help but notice that his arse was covered in an infestation of purple and yellow *boils!*

By the way, I was reliably informed soon after that Ginger was Maurice's wife, who was also…

A Mature Divinity student! *Revenge is mine, sayeth the Lord!*

It was, without doubt, the best night's craic I had ever had. Not to mention the goodnight kisses I received from the three good-looking girls, and of course, all the free beer!

PART 3
JOINING THE MICKS

CHAPTER 1

Back to work the next day, and the following weeks proved to be not so enjoyable. CS gas on the way into town, CS gas on the way home from town, and on occasions that were proving to be ever more frequent, sniper fire from across the rooftops, with bomb explosions increasing at an alarming rate, producing more and more casualties. Sometimes it was like living in the Wild West!

Businesses all over Belfast were suffering from the severe lack of daily custom and absolutely no one was buying fuckin' suits. All three branches of John Collier's, plus the two branches of our sister company i.e. Peter Pell's, were so far below in their retail targets it was only going to be a matter of time before something had to give. Then one morning at about eleven o'clock, a high-falutin' entourage appeared from our head office in Leeds: three directors and a wee fruit of a PA, who walked around as if he had a fuckin' cucumber stuck up his hole!

After the normal formalities Danny Lundy and the entourage made their way to the top floor, to the privacy of the staff rest room. About an hour later Danny appeared at his office, slightly agitated and obviously very upset. He called for me and another member of staff, Wee Joe, to inform us that the directors wished to speak to us on the second floor. When we arrived there, Wee Joe was taken by one of the directors into one of the two dressing rooms, while another of the directors took me into the second one at the other end of the floor.

There were no customers about so it felt as if there was deadly silence, then this smooth-talking oily wee fucker proceeded to tell me that due to lack of business in the shop, cuts would have to be made and I would be given a week's pay in lieu of notice; therefore my services were no longer required. In his words, *'Last in, first out!'*

I felt as if I had lost a fuckin' fiver and found a fuckin' pound! As I made my way towards the stairs I met Wee Joe who had been given the same bad news, and we both made our way down onto the first floor with the third director and the wee fruit of a PA walking slightly behind us. Maybe they thought we were going to wreck the shop; I didn't know and didn't really care.

We approached the office to say our goodbyes to Danny, who I believe was told to make the said cuts, but he refused to nominate anyone and the dirty work would have to be done by those on high i.e. the bearers of the bad news from Leeds.

When we told him of our demise, all hell broke loose when the cavalry arrived in the shape of Kate the cashier, who was also the fuckin' shop steward! My God, I couldn't believe what happened next!

Kate was on the 'phone as quick as a flash, informing the other four branches *(2 John Collier's and 2 Peter Pell's),* that all members of staff were to stop work immediately and make their way to the Union Office in Lower Garfield Street for an immediate meeting regarding the sacking of Wee Joe and me. Within about twenty minutes we were all gathered at the Union Office, with Kate holding court awaiting the arrival of our Head Honcho from the Belfast branch of the Union of Shop Workers.

I have to say how surprised I was at the swift reaction of my work colleagues from both Peter Pell's and John Collier's, and from all five branches, and the surprise from the management i.e. Danny Lundy, the directors and the wee fruit of a PA, at the speed at which we all vacated the three-floor shop, with customers in mid-flow in the Bespoke and Readymade suit sections left high and dry!

Danny was doing his best to accommodate the gobsmacked customers, with the directors and the wee fruit attempting to stand in for the sales staff and do you know, from what I could see, none of the clowns from the Leeds Head Office had a fuckin' clue!

I'm not sure but I think I caught Danny with a wee smile on his face or, possibly, trying not to laugh. I often wondered, after the event, how Kate had managed to organise everything so efficiently and so quickly! Anyway, the union rep showed up and it was quite obvious to all concerned that the fat fucker, with nothing on him that fitted, had ever worked in a multiple tailors environment. I think somebody said that he used to work in the delivery yard at one of the major department stores in town; probably sweeping up by the fuckin' look of him!

He fannied about for a while then Kate stood up and spoke for us all. She was like a woman possessed, I'm not fuckin' kiddin'. The only other woman I could compare her with in later years was Maggie Thatcher! Kate then dictated our strategy to the fat fucker, who then made a few hasty 'phone calls to seek advice from some other useless jobsworth penpusher, but in the end, the union agreed that if the situation was not resolved before the end of that day's trading, a ballot for an all-out strike would then be carried out, resulting in the necessary action being implemented with immediate effect! Leeds Head Office couldn't believe their ears when they were informed. Incidentally, no-one found the need to inform any of our branches around Belfast.

Now, bear in mind that all five of the shops concerned were manned by less than skeleton staff, and the main three-storey shop had Danny and the Prats from Leeds trying to make ends meet *(I would love to have been a fly on the wall!).*

It was just before lunch break that our walkout had taken place so all five shops, although quiet enough, if they were going to be busy, then over that period of time would be tested, to say the least.

I couldn't believe it when I found out later from Danny via Kate that it was the busiest the main branch had been for weeks! The Prats from Leeds were like headless chickens, with some customers walking out and, on two occasions, other customers asking for the names of the sales staff, i.e. the directors, to complain about their total lack of knowledge and severe lack of customer care. Oh, and by the way, the wee fruit of a PA who was made responsible for the cash office almost had a nervous breakdown, ran to the lift in tears, made his way to the top floor to hide in the staff rest room, meeting Jimmy Magee *(the tailor)* and his staff making their way down in the lift to join us in support of our industrial action, making life even more difficult for the Prats!

At about four o'clock a decision was made by the visiting directors, in conjunction with the Head Office in Leeds, that Wee Joe and I would be reinstated immediately and any cutbacks would be shelved for the foreseeable future. By the time we all got back to work it was nearly five o'clock, and according to the other four branch staff members, their shops had been in such disarray that each individual manager decided to close early to tidy up the mess.

When I arrived back at the main branch with the remainder of my workmates, the scene was almost indescribable. The Prats and the Wee Fruit made a hasty withdrawal, and when we arrived at the cash office on the first floor, Danny was sitting on his favourite chair with his feet resting on the cash desk, with a big mug of tea in one hand and a cigarette in the other. Kate immediately began to tidy up and without a word from anyone, the remainder of the staff followed suit, with Jimmy Magee and his staff helping out and Jimmy, in turn, locating the keys and locking the front door. It was with smiles, nods of reassurance and the general consensus of opinion that on that day there had been, indeed, a job well done.

Our unofficial motto from then onwards was: *don't mess with the best!*

Throughout the coming months and into the summer of 1970, businesses in and around the city centre began to pick up trade. More importantly, my commission was edging ahead of some of the other, more experienced staff. This would sometimes lead to my superiors sending me to carry out mundane jobs in quiet periods so as the senior salesmen could monopolize what trade was available. Danny was aware that my expertise in salesmanship was beginning to upset a chosen few so he came up with an excellent idea to remedy the situation.

Now, not everyone working in our shops was lucky enough to live as close to work as I did. Due to the ongoing troubles, public transport was often late or didn't operate at all; consequently there were a lot of days when a certain amount of staff couldn't get to work or arrived in very late. That's where I came in! Danny used me as a roaming relief on the three floors in our shop and in the other two John Collier's shops in town. This meant that I became familiar with not just the main three-storey shop in Royal Avenue but with the other two one-storey shops, one in Ann Street and the other in North Street, all within easy walking distance for me. This led to me being involved in a lot more trading, resulting in a lot more commission. Danny advised me not to brag too much about my new-found wealth but as he explained to certain individuals, I was prepared to go to any shop at short notice, even on my day off, re-familiarise myself with the layout, and trade as if I was a permanent member of that shop's staff! Things were really on the up and up for me, not just because I was earning good money but because I actually enjoyed doing what I did for a living.

My drumming was improving all the time and the Pipe Band was picking up more paid gigs. My visits to Queens' increased to two nights a week, and sometimes I would be invited to take part in a jamming session at one of the many students' venues around the centre of town. The Lyric Youth Theatre was playing a vital part in my life. I learned something new there every week, plus, of course, mixing with such a cross-section of the community didn't do my confidence any harm at all. I couldn't help but wonder about the reason for my dramatic improvement in sales technique. Long may it continue!

Brian McAleese and I had a lot of fun in his car. We travelled the length and breadth of Ireland, sometimes with the Gang of Four, sometimes just the two of us. On one occasion Brian and I decided to drive down to Dublin for an overnight stay, using Robert and Anne's house as a base. Some of our friends thought that it was a bit far but I can honestly say that a night away from the Belfast War was, without doubt, a most enjoyable experience.

We had a great night out in Dublin, and a long lie-in the following morning, followed by a humungous breakfast before being sent off to Mass by Anne. After the usual huge Sunday dinner and the obligatory snooze, we set off for home with the sun shining and not a care in the world.

About thirty minutes into our journey, we spotted two lovely wee hitchhikers with two equally lovely wee arses! They were heading for Newry which, of course, was on our way.

Two wee blonde bombshells with tight-fitting jeans! We turned the car radio up, Brian put his foot to the floor and the two girls were suitably impressed. They had also been in Dublin the previous night to see their favourite show band, Dickie Rock and the Miami. In those days the Miami Show Band was renowned for being the absolute best in show band music. They were telling us all about the great night out they'd had, but had to save up for ages to get the money to go, and of course had to rely on lifts to and from the venue. Luckily for them, they were able to stay with a relative, but the thought of the journey back home with rain forecast later that day had been a worry to say the least; they really appreciated us giving them a lift. Brian and I glanced at each other, hoping that the girls would find a special way of thanking us. It wasn't long before we were all smoking, joking and laughing as if we had been friends for years. Not far from Newry we pulled into a filling station to fuel up and get a cold drink. This was our chance to spend a couple of bob and spoil the girls, to sort of seal our new-found friendship. When we got back into the car, I jumped into the back seat with one of the girls allowing the other girl to take the front passenger seat. So far so good; no one complained. After a wee smooch, with Brian eyeballing me through the rearview mirror, he pulled over to a secluded spot and proceeded to swop spit with the other girl; then the unforgivable happened.

The girl with Brian let one rip!!! Rip? It was like fuckin' cannon fire! She fuckin' stank to fuck! Brian began to cough and, would you believe it, up came the packet of Tayto and Coke he had at the filling station! Bearing in mind we were in a two-door Triumph Herald, I was trying to get from the back seat over the top of the Stinker From Hell, and just get some fresh air, being more than hindered by my smooching partner who, at this stage, was threatening to join Brian in the vomit department. Finally, we all managed to get out of the car with the Stinker still going strong, Brian wiping the puke from the front of his pullover and trousers with girl number two, and me standing at the back of the car. Brian then began a tirade of insults and swearing that should have gone down in the history books! Unfortunately I started to get a fit of the giggles which did nothing to help the situation and made Brian even more exasperated than he already was. Thankfully, girl number two waved down a passing bus that was going into Newry town centre. Both girls quickly got on board the bus and that was the last we saw of them! Brian and I eventually got back inside the car and decided a smoke was in order. The cigarettes that we normally kept on the dashboard had vanished and we had spent the last of our money at the filling station! Bastardin' bitches!!!

Back to the grindstone at John Collier's with trade improving on a daily basis. Many more people were venturing into the city centre, taking advantage of a lull in the hostilities whenever they dared to do so. There was no guarantee that if it was a quiet morning without the expected explosions, rifle or gun fire, and false alarms via the telephone to the police or the media, that it would be a quiet afternoon. Therefore, you paid your money and took your chances like everybody else!

My work colleagues and I would often make a small wager to see who could guess what street or road the latest explosion had taken place in. If the blast was some distance away then the closest guess to that general area would win the bet. The whole scenario became almost surreal!

On one particular afternoon I was sent with the bottom half of a mannequin to the Ann Street branch for use by the company window-dressers, who were doing their usual rounds of seasonal fashion change. It was a custom to cover the arse bit with wrapping paper but it was obvious what I had under my arm, especially with the bus and taxi drivers! Wolf whistles and sexual innuendoes were the favourites on every occasion, but I was still the junior of juniors and at least it gave the rest of the shop staff a chance to fit a couple of good sales in while I was away.

On the way there I met Sammy, a friend of mine who worked in a shoe shop in High Street. He was tasked with taking a bag of change to another of his branches in Royal Avenue. We stopped for a wee yarn outside a large electrical shop with some sort of office complex on the upper floors. There were always good-looking girls and the odd good-looking older woman going in and out so it was a great spot to do some leching! Anyway, after satisfying our adolescent cravings we went on our merry way to carry out our tasks. While I was in the Ann Street shop, an almighty explosion occurred that rocked the very foundations of the building! The manager said, *"Fuck me! That was fuckin' close!"*

He then instructed me to get back to the main branch as quickly as possible for fear that more of the same was to follow. On my way back I ran into Sammy again in High Street, on the opposite side of the street where we were standing earlier, where we both greeted each other with dropped jaws. The building where we were carrying out our usual leching was blown to smithereens! Men and women were screaming in agony, grief and absolute shock at the devastation they found themselves in.

Emergency services quickly arrived on the scene. Bodies were being carried out, some covered in blood and dust, some alive, some dead, some with arms or legs missing. Complete mayhem swiftly followed, with Sammy and me physically shaking, and tears beginning to run down Sammy's face. Had that bomb gone off fifteen minutes earlier, we would undoubtedly have been among the casualties! We both reassured each other and, once again, went our separate ways and returned to our place of work.

When I arrived back at the main branch just a few minutes later, several more bombs went off around the centre of town. At this stage I was finding it extremely difficult to take everything in as this was the closest to any atrocity that I had ever been. In the past I had always been at a distance or managed to arrive close to the scene sometime later. It was then I realised that, in fact, I was covered in dust. My suit jacket looked like it had been hanging somewhere for a very long time without being brushed or dusted. My work colleagues made me a cup of tea and Danny insisted I sit down in his office under the watchful eye of Kate while my jacket was sorted out. My hands were still shaking and I had to work overtime to prevent myself from crying. Danny allowed me to go home early.

He said, *"Straight home ney, do ya hear me!"*

I slept very little that night. Flashes of what I had witnessed that day kept my mind constantly buzzing until dawn. Once again I was up for work before Mammy, and I have to confess I decided to tell her what had happened the previous day. She found it difficult to comprehend just how close she came to losing me. Mammy also included Sammy and his parents in her deliberations, and also in her prayers of thanks to 'yer man upstairs' for keeping us both safe.

Although trade dropped off for a while, it wasn't long before it picked up again with a vengeance. There seemed to be a dogged determination with the Belfast people to carry on regardless. The general public needed to go into town and shop, needed to earn a living, needed to put food on the table, needed to look forward to Christmas and the New Year.

And the whole time I couldn't help but wonder how long would they put up with it? I for one was beginning to make plans to leave Belfast; no, not just Belfast, but leave Northern Ireland. What would Mammy say?

More days, more weeks, more months of non-ending emotional turmoil. Walking on eggs, walking on thin ice, walking on a perennial time-bomb! Did anybody outside Northern Ireland really know how we were surviving, how on earth we made ends meet, how in God's name we got up every morning and faced another day of uncertainty, of forsakenness, of total abandonment; of fuckin' bollix!!!

Belfast city centre became a ghost town after about nine o'clock every night, such was the fear within the local population of venturing beyond the confines of their own neighbourhood. Someone once said that Belfast at night was like a graveyard with traffic lights! However, this fact of life didn't always deter me.

After one of my many visits to Queens', I was walking home at about eleven o'clock via the main bus route into town, ensuring I stayed away from any short-cuts through the side streets. By doing this I didn't stray into any gangs who may be keeping an eye on their local turf. Buses were few and far between but it was a pleasant night and the streets were pretty quiet. As I made my way around the City Hall and along Donegal Street, I couldn't believe how unusually quiet it was. Although there was plenty of street lighting, the shadows in shop doorways and street corners were beginning to make me jumpy. Occasionally I found the need to glance over my shoulder then hurry a wee bit, trying not to make too much noise, by gently trotting across any roads or streets in my path. I took a left up Castle Street and I knew once I passed St Mary's school, I would be almost home and dry. As I was passing Lipton's Supermarket I just had to stop for a moment and take hold of myself, ponder for a while in the shelter of the main doors, assuring myself that I wasn't being followed and if I was; what was I going to fuckin' do anyway?

I decided to have a wee smoke, just to calm my nerves. No, I thought, better not. Someone might see the glow of the cigarette and claim me if there was nobody else available! I took a deep breath and the intake of the smell of stale urine almost made me puke.

'Is there no fuckin' end to this fuckin' hell?'

Another attempt at a deep breath and once again I was on the move, promising myself that I would look neither left, right or backwards. I could see the lights of Divis Tower in the distance, smiled with relief and put an extra inch in my step. It was amazingly quiet and still. Yes, amazingly quiet; and still... *baaaang!!!!!*

An explosion took place not far behind me, almost knocking me off my feet; then the cracking sound of automatic fire. I turned and saw that Hasting Street Barracks was being attacked by a number of armed men, who were also throwing petrol bombs at the main facade of the building. I immediately jumped into the nearest doorway and very quickly found myself crouched down in the foetal position. For what seemed like an eternity, but I learned later was only about five minutes, I said as many Hail Marys and Our Fathers as possible with one mouth!

As soon as the noise died down, I was up in a flash, another deep breath, didn't panic; took my time making the remaining short distance home without drawing attention to myself thus not giving the Security Forces the impression that I may have been involved in the attack. This was a very wise move as there were police and soldiers all over the place; not just from within the Barracks but from the surrounding area.

Inside, the main entrance hall of Divis Tower was packed full of many of the tenants who had made their way there to ogle the scene, and other passers-by who had sought a safe haven when the attack was taking place. I bulldozed my way through the crowd and into the lift which took me up to the eleventh floor and home to Mammy and Paddy. Mammy asked, *"Did you see what happened, son?"* I replied, *"Ach, Mammy, same old, same old."*

I went to my room, threw my anorak on the chair beside my bed, then realised that I was covered in sweat and my shirt was absolutely soaking! My hands were shaking again, my mind was rushing back and forward again. I was replaying the whole scene over and over, again and again. That one word was beginning to haunt me: *again! Again! Again!*

My personal near-misses were becoming alarmingly more frequent. I thought that it was only going to be a matter of time before I was picked up by a rival group, whereupon I would be lucky to see the next light of day, or caught up in some sort of explosion or crossfire! Nail biting became an uncontrollable urge, twenty-four seven! The whole situation in Northern Ireland, with Belfast getting more than its fair share of atrocities was,

A total fuckin' nightmare!!!

But what in hell could anybody do about it? Absolutely nothing! But what I found extremely difficult to comprehend was the fact that Joe Public carried on in everyday life, as if there was no other alternative worth considering. How the fuck does that work? Was I the only person in Belfast who could not and would not entertain this form of existence, for that's exactly what it was: an existence, not a lifestyle. Were we that fuckin' thick? Maybe we were!

Anyway, as 1970 progressed towards the festive season, I couldn't help but wonder how great Christmas and New Year were in the past and how those great times were slowly but surely becoming distant memories, so on one of my days off I decided to do something about it. I knew that I wanted to move from Belfast, and after considering Dublin and London, I knew within myself that I would need to travel further afield, to escape the genuine depression that I felt because of the unending troubles in my native land. As far away as possible to escape the daily newspapers and television coverage of the ongoing bitterness between two communities who showed no intention of settling their differences for a long time to come. If I could just get away for a while, just to try to get my head around the whole situation… Ah fuck, who was I kidding? I just wanted to get *out!* Yes, get out and as far away as possible.

My brother Pat had mentioned to me on several occasions about joining the Irish Guards. I had considered following in Frank's and

Robert's footsteps and joining the Irish Army but at my young age, almost seventeen, the chances of me going abroad with the Irish Army, who were deployed in several locations in the Middle East, were pretty remote. However, the Micks were posted to Hong Kong!

Now, wouldn't that be far enough away from all the troubles in Belfast, and, of course, wouldn't that be one hell of an adventure? As I said earlier, on one of my days off I decided to do something about it, and made my way to the Army Careers Office in York Street, where I met a man who helped to change my life forever.

When I arrived at the office I stood for a while and glanced at the posters in the window with, I have to say, more than just a wee bit of apprehension. A man of about forty-odd came out to the front door, dressed in a shirt, tie, dark trousers with black shiny shoes, and commented on the fair weather we were having for that time of year. He kindly offered me a cigarette, gave me a light, and continued in some light banter until I let slip that I had always wanted to travel, and how grand some of the uniforms in the window presentation looked. He then invited me in to the main office, and within a few moments his younger colleague produced two mugs of tea with a plate of chocolate biscuits. The younger colleague was equally well-dressed and as equally polite as the older, and before long all three of us were swopping jokes, refilling the mugs, and I was certainly hoofing the chocolate biscuits away like there was no tomorrow. Several other work colleagues came and went with all of them addressing the man who invited me in as 'sir'. I thought he must be the boss and also very important. I was to learn later that he was CSM Allister *(Company Sergeant Major)* and in charge of the Belfast Army Careers Office. When I met him some years later he had been promoted to RSM Allister *(Regimental Sergeant Major)* and was in charge of recruiting for the whole of Northern Ireland and the Republic of Ireland.

After spending about an hour in the office, CSM Allister couldn't believe his ears when I confirmed that I was the younger brother of Pat McCann, whom he knew very well indeed. I thought he was going to start dancing on a fuckin' bass drum! The other guys in the office were, as it were, very impressed and couldn't do enough for me. Anyway, after completing a simple written test, a further appointment was made for me to return with my parents, as I was under the age of eighteen and would need their written consent to join the Army.

When I arrived home on that particular day, Mammy and Paddy couldn't help noticing the huge grin on my face. When I explained where I had been, neither of them seemed in the least bit surprised and wanted to be given all the relevant details, which I was duly delighted to supply. Mammy was sitting all prim and proper, especially when I told her how well Pat had been referred to and how much respect the people in the Careers Office had for him. Paddy told me that Mammy and he had spoken quite often about how long it would be before I followed in my sibling's footsteps and decided to leave home for pastures new. They were both delighted to accompany me at my next appointment two weeks later. In the meantime I would need two references, a task Mammy took on, and within only a few days I had the very same sitting in nice official brown envelopes; one from our parish priest and the other from my primary school headmaster, who was now headmaster at St Comgall's just round the corner. Both referees expressed to Mammy their admiration and also their concern for my chosen profession, but also added that at least I was looking for a way to improve my lifestyle and escape the whirlpool of daily violence, CS gas and barricaded streets.

The next two weeks couldn't pass quick enough, as I was naive enough to think that they might change their minds in the Careers Office! I needn't have worried, for as soon as we arrived CSM

Allister and his staff were ready and waiting, treating Mammy and Paddy like Lord and Lady Muck!

Fuck me! Out came the chocolate biscuits again, and this time not the normal mugs for tea, but lovely china cups, saucers and side plates! Well, I have to say, everything went very smoothly, with Mammy and Paddy thinking they had won a day out at fuckin' Stormont!

Due to the close proximity of the festive season, a medical was arranged for early January 1971 and Mammy duly supplied all the details of our local doctor so that he could be contacted, if necessary, before or after that examination.

The only thing that worried Mammy was the fact that after I completed my training, I would be given a spot of leave and then travel to the other side of the world to Hong Kong, and be there for a period of about fifteen months without getting back home, with the only contact being letters or cards. Paddy also nodded in agreement when the subject of homesickness came up, to which I protested that I would be enjoying myself in Hong Kong far too bloody much to worry about bloody Belfast! My mini-outburst took everyone present by surprise, but thankfully it remedied the situation; for the time being anyway. At the end of what was a very productive appointment, CSM Allister arranged for one of his colleagues to give us a lift home to Divis Tower, to the absolute delight of Mammy and Paddy. That Allister fella certainly knew how to lay it on, thick and fast!

When we arrived home there were a few of our neighbours, standing in and around the corner shop at the bottom of Divis Tower, who couldn't help but notice all the attention that our chauffeur was expending, particularly on Mammy. I could only surmise the out-of-earshot comments that would have been exchanged.

*"Who the hell does she think she is? Can't bloody walk like the rest of us, **fuckin' cow!**"*

However, on reflection, I had empathy for our driver's point-blank refusal to come up to our flat in Divis Tower for a wee cup of tea. Mammy said, *"He must have been in a hurry to get home, God love him."* My thoughts on the subject in later years were *'There but for the grace of God go I'.*

New Year came with a bang; quite a few bangs actually, normal for Belfast!

My medical went like a dream and all the other paperwork was completed over a short period of time. A few weeks later Mammy and Paddy received a letter asking them to once more accompany me to the Careers Office to sign the consent forms and to be reassured by everyone there that their wee Brendan would be well looked after. The final blessing was secured by the fact that Pat was posted as an instructor to the Guards Depot, Pirbright, in Surrey, where I would be carrying out my basic training. Would this be a very good or a very bad thing?

At least, if I didn't like it or was feeling homesick I would have a shoulder to cry on. Little did Mammy and Paddy know that our Pat would be the last fucker to let anyone cry on his fuckin' shoulder! Least of all his wee fuckin' brother!

But I've got to say if I was honest with myself, I knew, hand on heart, I wouldn't have had it any other fuckin' way! I thought to myself *'When I eventually get there, they can bring it fuckin' on!'*

The next thing on the agenda was my disembarkation date. With St Patrick's Day fast approaching, including lots of paid gigs with the Pipe Band before and after the great day, and Easter just around the next corner with an equal amount of commitments including an assortment of indoor and outdoor performances, it was mutually agreed that I would give my notice to John Collier's just before the

Easter break and leave for Pirbright via the Heysham boat on Easter Wednesday, expecting to arrive at Pirbright sometime on Easter Thursday. Well, I was glad we got that lot sorted!

I have to say that Danny Lundy, my boss at John Collier's, was very surprised at my decision to join the Army, but also expressed a great sense of disappointment at losing the most potential young branch manager that he had ever seen. I could hardly believe my fuckin' ears! On several occasions he sat me down in his office and actually asked me if my parents and I had thought the whole thing through. One of his most memorable comments was,

"Brendan, if you stay with this company, you could be a branch manager by the time you are twenty-one." On one such occasion, I nearly had a wee tear in me eye.

Although I assured the Pipe Band that I would be available for all our gigs up to Easter Week, just about every drummer and piper, including the pipe major and drum major, and of course our leading tip Eamonn, offered what they thought were good reasons for not leaving Belfast. *"Do you really think that you'll like it in the Army?"* This was a question that cropped up time and time again.

The next port of call to make my bold announcement was the Lyric Youth Theatre. After successfully completing a two-year sponsored course, the news of my impending departure went down like a lead balloon! At first I thought they may have been pissed off with me for wasting all that time and money. However, a letter from Mrs O'Malley *(the O'Malleys were the head honchos of the Arts Council in Belfast)* arrived at our door in Divis Tower only a few days after I had made known my intentions to my tutors and fellow thespians. The letter was addressed to Mammy, and when she opened up the pure white, slightly thicker-than-normal envelope and produced the pure white, slightly thicker-than-normal writing paper, she looked as if she was turning equally pure white. My initial thought was that she had been sent a huge bill for my two-year course at the Lyric Youth Theatre!

Mammy read the letter to herself several times before she sat down to read it aloud for Paddy and me. I couldn't have been more wrong. The content of the letter was so complimentary regarding my progress, my enthusiasm, and the uncorked talent that I apparently had that was just about ready for fruition! Could she *(Mammy)* not persuade me to change my mind? Mrs O'Malley also suggested that if I was to move to any other location in the British Isles, then she *(Mrs O'Malley)* would recommend me to an appropriate Theatre Group to continue my progression. I think Hong Kong was probably outside her remit.

Mammy and Paddy gave me one of those *'are you sure?'* looks. I looked straight back at them and said that although no one wanted me to go, for very valid reasons, I'd made up my mind and that Hong Kong was too much of a temptation not to give it a good go!

I have to say at this point, Mammy thought so much of Mrs O'Malley's letter that I do believe she kept it until her dying day!

As my departure from John Collier's drew closer, I worked every available day, and sold every available item to every available customer, especially the men when they had a few jars who would sometimes take anything home to keep the wife off their backs. When the wives brought the offending item and the then sober husband back for a replacement, I fiddled the books so as I got awarded commission on both occasions. By the time anyone found out I would be long gone. Piece of cake! The money I made from the paid gigs with the Pipe Band was also saved for my last few days at home. My rationale was quite simple: earn as much money as possible so as I could party like hell before leaving Belfast, and squander the rest on my journey to Pirbright. *I'm yer fuckin' man!*

CHAPTER 2

A FTER WHAT SEEMED LIKE A PERIOD OF never-ending parties and goodbyes, my last day at home finally arrived. I was due at the Careers Office on Wednesday 24th April 1971 to collect my documentation for travelling, and about £3.50 cash, which was a bonus as I hadn't realised that I would be paid in advance. While I was there I met another potential Mick from Dublin called Tony Kerrigan. CSM Allister asked if I could look after him for the day as he didn't want him wandering around town on his own, and after all, it was his first time in Belfast. Another Dubliner called John Cunningham who was delayed, would be travelling with us and we would meet him that night on the boat.

Anyway, off I went with my new-found friend, gave him a quick tour of the city centre and soon arrived back at Divis Tower, where Mammy and Paddy made Tony extremely welcome. After a great feed of steak, spuds, onions and gravy washed down with a lovely glass of milk, Mammy made up two bundles of sandwiches for us to eat on our travels. After a handshake from Paddy, a kiss and a great big hug from Mammy, Tony and I made our way into town to have a few drinks with my mates who worked in the shops around the city centre. There was about a dozen or so, male and female, all gathered in the Deer's Head in North Street. Tony felt a wee bit out of his depth at first but after a couple of drinks he really enjoyed the craic. Once again I did the rounds of goodbyes, handshakes, hugs and kisses from well-puckered lips of the girls who weren't afraid to stick the odd tongue halfway down my throat. Tony loved the kissing bit especially as he had never met any of the girls before. I remember he said something like: *"Jasus, Brendan, they'er really friendly up heore."*

At about nine o'clock that night we found ourselves in the queue to board the Heysham boat. I knew, because of our midweek sailing, that the boat shouldn't be too packed but I told Tony we should find a table in the bar as soon as possible, just in case. That was also the likeliest place where we would meet up with John, our fellow traveller. True to form, as soon as the bar opened it was packed! Although there was no live band that night there was a juke box with a great variety of music, and it wasn't long before Tony spotted John, whereupon we all got slightly bladdered, to say the least.

As the night wore on, I advised my two travelling companions of the dos and don'ts of both the boat and train journeys that lay before us, particularly regarding the unnecessary flashing of the cash they were carrying. They were both very grateful and our subsequent travels went without a hitch. When we arrived at Euston Station in London I was very quick to point out the best route across London, using the Underground to Waterloo Station and then onwards to Brookwood in Surrey. Well, when Tony and John saw this huge map of the Underground system on the wall, they just stood there open-mouthed and completely dumbfounded. To be fair, I had been lucky enough to use the Underground on many previous occasions so it was up to me to make sure we got to our final destination in one piece. Tony and John couldn't have been more appreciative and insisted that, any time we had a drink or a bite to eat, they should pay. John reckoned that had he and Tony been travelling without a chief scout, they would have been AWOL *(Absent without leave)* before they even started.

Eventually we arrived at Brookwood Station. We were the only passengers to alight from the train, and after receiving directions from the ticket collector we walked the short distance to the bus stop, ensuring that we did not loiter in the area of the Brookwood Arms, immediately opposite the station! Better not chance fate; still slightly hung over from the previous night's partying, drink taken would not be one of my best ideas. On arrival at the bus stop, none of us could make head nor tail of the badly damaged timetable hanging on by its last legs to the bus shelter, so we once again received directions from the ticket collector who was on his way home for lunch. It was a bright sunny day as we began the last leg of our journey, about a thirty-minute walk to our final destination: the Guards Depot!

The main entrance had two large barriers controlling the access, manned by two equally large men in uniform, with grand hats with shiny peaks that almost covered their eyes. They gave us that up and down look, and some hasty directions that I could only understand by their hand movements as their accents, one Scottish, the other Welsh, were that thick you could have sliced them in half with a fuckin' bread knife!

As we strolled through this huge Army Camp with so much going on, at first nobody gave us a second glance. There were people flying about as if the end of the world was just around the corner, and we must have stood out like sore thumbs, with various inmates of various shapes and sizes, offering the odd snigger, knowing glances and a cupped-hand gesture of up and down movements, miming the word 'wankers', to help us on our way. After about fifteen minutes of uncertainty and all three of us wondering what in God's name had we let ourselves in for, we arrived at the Receiving Room. This was an office complex with onsite accommodation, showers, toilets etc. where our final processing would take place. We spent our first forty-eight hours there and quickly made friends with another three potential Micks, all from the Waterside in Derry. We were fed and watered at the nearby cookhouse (one of two in Camp), but unfortunately for us, every other department we had to go to was at the other side of camp, including the clothing stores where we received our *ginormous* initial issue of kit. You should have seen the state of us carrying all this fuckin' stuff all the way back across camp to the Receiving Room, just to carry the whole fuckin' lot back through camp to our training accommodation the following fuckin' day!

Anyway, when we got to our barrack room we were greeted by several other Mick recruits who we would be joining for basic training starting on Monday morning. Most had arrived before Easter, but due to lack of numbers they weren't allowed to begin training until we three and the other three from N. Ireland had showed up, so those jammy bastards had a long weekend off over Easter with pay, plus a head start on settling in while the last six arrivals had a lot to do before Monday morning. Any concerns we may have had were quickly put to rest, as everyone to a man chipped in to help out, and after only twenty-four hours, I felt as if I had known everyone in that room for years. My adventure had well and truly begun in earnest!

The basic training was fast and furious, but believe it or not, I really enjoyed it. Every day was a challenge, full of never-ending changes, surprises, fastballs and downright embuggerance factors! We were all guilty of laughing at the most ridiculous and unbelievable scenarios we found ourselves in, on a daily basis. The Mick recruits were as follows:

Myself	Belfast
'Bronco' Campbell	Belfast
Bobby 'Stewarty' Stewart	Belfast
'Lexy' Wallace	Derry/Londonderry/The Walled City
Ian Cresswell	Derry/Londonderry/The Walled City
Terry Edwards	Derry/Londonderry/The Walled City

Joe Coyle	Letterkenny
Tony Kerrigan	Dublin
John Cunningham	Dublin
Micky Melia	Bray
Pete Gallagher	Liverpool
Jimmy Walsh	Liverpool
'Soup' Campbell	Birmingham
Colin Sampson	London

Add to this lot about eight Welsh Guard recruits with names like Evans, Roberts, Jones etc., who, although based in separate accommodation to ours, joined our squad each day for training to make up the appropriate numbers. Basic training included:square-bashing, weapon training, live firing, map-reading, field-craft, basic PT, circuit training, battle PT, assault course competition, swimming, shining parades (which meant personal kit cleaning, in silence, and speaking only when spoken to about matters concerning Regimental History), and the dreaded Early Morning Room And Locker Inspections!

It was a great asset for all of us to have a form of inter-regimental competition; up close and personal every day, but still maintaining a team atmosphere against any outsiders looking in. This meant that we could slag off each other but no one outside our squad was allowed to do so. Those Welsh boys certainly gave us Micks a good run for our money, particularly in the singing stakes!

The Mick training staff that dealt with our squad on most occasions were as follows:

CSM Tommy Corcoron	Dublin
Sgt Paddy McCann	Belfast, and my brother
Sgt Willy McClernon	Belfast
Sgt Bob Allister	Belfast, and brother of CSM Allister in the Army Careers Office

L/Sgt 'Hovis' Browne	Dublin
L/Sgt Vince McEllin	Mayo
L/Sgt Paddy Green	Belfast

There were also two stores staff known as:

| 'Fitzy' | Dublin. |
| 'Hairy Doc' | Castlederg, and brother of Séamus Doherty, Maura's husband. |

There were a number of other staff that assisted us on our way, but I have to give a special mention to 'Hovis' Browne and Vince McEllin, who were with us every painstaking step of the way, from start to finish! Two professional heartbreakers!

After ten weeks of training which included two long weekends, both of which I spent in London visiting my brothers and sisters and really living it up, I asked Mammy to send me some civvies (civilian clothing). I had a few bits and pieces but nothing that made me stand out in a crowd. Within about ten days two parcels arrived, each containing shirts, ties, shoes, socks, underpants, a sports jacket and slacks, one twopiece and one threepiece suit. On my next night out to Guildford, I was sure that I would make a dynamic impression. For any lucky Oul One *(young lady)* I would look like a long-awaited but well-deserved dessert! We were usually allowed out from about four o'clock to midnight on a Saturday night, so I wanted to spread as much whoopie as possible! That's me, generous to a fault!

Chapter 3

A FEW WEEKS LATER OUR TRAINING SQUAD moved from our initial accommodation to the other side of camp, to a location not far from the Receiving Room, two more robust and slightly more old-fashioned barrack rooms. This was the first time both the Micks and the Welsh would all be together twenty-four seven, and we had progressed to being referred to as a platoon rather than a squad *(a sort of communal promotion)*. This area was known as D Lines and was much closer to the training area where we would progress in our Field Training, etcetera.

Covered in muck and dirt, wet and cold, digging in, hounded up and down hills, racing over the thirty-two-obstacle assault course on numerous occasions, live firing day and night, in a final bid to turn us all into Guardsmen! The upside of this part of our training was that we would leave the drill square behind until our passing out parade, which would take place at the end of our course, which was fast approaching. Also left behind were the shining parades and the dreaded early morning room and locker inspections.

Anyway, on the last Saturday night we had off before making our way to the battle camp at Thetford for our final make-or-break manoeuvres, we all made plans to meet up in Guildford in the Royal, everyone's favourite disco pub.

Now, because we would be away early the following morning and I didn't want to leave anything to chance, not knowing what the training staff would have in store for us on our immediate arrival at Thetford, I decided to double-check everything and get a slightly later bus to Guildford. Being very pleased with myself that I had left no stone unturned and was fully prepared for anything that would come my way the next morning, I togged myself out in my three-piece brown suit, bright yellow shirt, silk tie with matching silk hanky in my top jacket pocket and a pair of highly polished dark brown shoes. Oh yes; and a nice wee fancy pair of cufflinks, with dark socks being an absolute must!!!

Of course, being so close to completing my training I had developed a wee bit of a Mick swagger as I perambulated out of D Lines, down the main road with all the sprogs *(those still in the early stage of squad training)* springing to attention as I passed them, mistaking *me* for a member of *staff!* I could see the Guard Room in the distance and was so sure that I would impress the bollixes of whoever was on duty, they might even let slip a word of praise for my *eeeemaculate* turnout!

When I arrived at the window of the Guard Room to book out for the night, I was greeted by the Sergeant on duty with a big, big smile, who just couldn't help himself but comment on my city-slicker outfit. Then the gobshite dropped the fuckin' bombshell.

He said, *"Where's yer hanky?"*

I said, *"I've a lovely silk one, Sergeant, in me top pocket."*

He said, *"That's not a proper hanky. It's only for show. Now fuck off back to yer barrack room and get a proper fuckin' hanky."*

So off I went with me tail between me legs, legging it like fuck so as I would still have time to catch the next bus to Guildford. When I finally returned to the Guard Room, there were small beads of sweat beginning to appear on my forehead and I was slightly out of breath.

I said, *"Here's me hanky, Sergeant."*

He said, *"It's not fuckin' ironed. Now fuck off back to yer barrack room and get it fuckin' ironed.'"*

I said, *"Fuck this for a game of cowboys" (under me breath).*

So off I went, prayin' te God that the fuckin' arsehole Sergeant would fall over and knock himself fuckin' out!

After another return journey at breakneck speed, I finally, hopefully finally, returned to the Guard Room, puffing and panting just a wee bit, whereupon I produced my nicely ironed, clean and proper hanky.

I said, *"Here's me hanky, Sergeant."*

He said, *"Well done, young McCann, but there's no point in bookin' out now."*

I said, *"Why not, Sergeant?"*

He said, *"Because you've just missed yer bus into Guildford! By the time you get the next one, it'll get ye there just in time to get the last bus back here!"*

I said, *"Well, thanks anyway, Sergeant. I'll just take a wee stroll over to the NAAFI Bar!"*

I've got to say, as I walked away from the Guard Room, I was spitting fuckin' feathers! All dressed up and nowhere to go. But hey, it was all part of the embuggerance factor. Oh yes, the Sergeant on duty who so desperately wanted to see my well-ironed hanky, well, he was none other than Sergeant Paddy McCann! The fuckin' gobshite!

When I got to the *NAAFI Bar* there was no one in there except the barmaid who, because it was such a quiet night, was pulling down the metal grill and closing early! She quickly suggested that I use the bar next door where her boyfriend and his mate were having a drink. After some serious consideration I decided, ah well, in for a penny, in for a pound, so off I went; into the corporals' mess!

As I walked through the main door of the mess, I was greeted by two L/Cpls in uniform who had been told of my arrival by the barmaid, and I was immediately offered a drink and asked who I was. There was no one else present so I decided to announce myself as L/Cpl Murphy of the Micks. I explained that I was posted in from London to start work on Monday morning but thought I would get there a couple of days early to suss the place out.

The much larger of the two was about six foot four and in the Grenadier Guards, with carrot-coloured hair and a face full of freckles. He said that although his name was Bobby, he was known to his mates as Ginge. His mate, who was just over six foot and in the Coldstream Guards, said that although his name was Andy, he was known to his mates as Geordie. I told them that although my name was Jimmy, I was known to my mates as Spud!

Well now, all three of us sat there having a fair oul drink with the barmaid giving us a couple of pints on the house and serving us well after time. You would have thought that Ginge, Geordie and Spud had been close friends for years and everything was being done to ensure that I felt at home in my new posting. I couldn't have asked for more, could I?

At about half past eleven Ginge and Geordie had to report to the Guard Room to assist with the booking-in of all the recruits that had gone out for the night. However, before they left the NAAFI they would have to lock the main doors. And there I was, thinking that I would be left behind with Ginge's Oul One! Then all of a sudden, Ginge suggested that since I had said that I was accommodated in the same block as him and Geordie, that I should walk his girlfriend over to his bunk on the top floor and wait for him and Geordie to join us for a nightcap.

I began to chant in the back of my mind *I'm Yer Man! I'm Yer Man! I'm Yer Man!*

Off the two groups went on their separate ways, with the Oul One and me making sure we kept to the shadows for fear anyone would spot us as it was not allowed to take females into male accommodation in those days. We needn't have worried for just about everyone who was on duty would be down at the Guard Room. In just a few short minutes we arrived at the foot of the stairs of the block with only the odd light on to assist us upwards and onwards to Ginge's bunk.

Of course at this stage, I had found out that her name was Daphne. I thought *'Fuckin' Daphne. What sort of a fuckin' name is that?'*

I also supplied a gentlemanly helping hand: One under each tit to be exact.

She was definitely game-on, and by the time we got into Ginge's bunk I was definitely on. Straight on to be exact! It didn't take long for us both to exchange bodily fluids, lie back and enjoy one of Ginge's cigarettes, sink one of his cans of beer, and for me to secretly admire my handy work of psychedelic love bites on both sides of her neck. And me, hey, I still had on me waistcoat, shirt, tie and shoes and socks!

I glanced at my watch. It was just about quarter past twelve. I decided to make a quick getaway as Ginge would soon be finished at the Guard Room and on his way back.

I crept out of the flea-pit that was supposed to be a bed. Fuck me! The sheets were like cardboard! Daphne was having a wee boozy doze with a very light, snottery snore accompanied by a wee whistle from her lips. Top or bottom lips? I wasn't too sure.

At this stage, in a moment of sheer lunacy, I decided a wee thank-you note for Ginge would be in order. I grabbed an old envelope and pen from the bedside locker, and the thought of the note that my brother Billy had left my brother Pat after pawning Pat's good suit all those years before, had me in stitches, and if I didn't hurry up, I'd be needing more than stitches when Ginge got back. If I remember rightly the note read as follows:

'Hi Ginge,

Thanks for the beer, thanks for the ciggy, thanks for the poke at Daphne!

Yer Friend Spud!'

Just as I was leaving the bunk, I heard the sound of boots coming up the stairs and a cockney accent bellowing out, *"Are you ready for me, darling? Ginge 'Arris is on his way. This is your lucky fucking day. I'm gonna ride 'em, cowboy; ride 'em, cowboy!!"*

My heart sank! I quickly sprang into the nearby toilets and hid in one of the cubicles, still trying to put my trousers on! Would you believe it, the big fucker came in for a slash.

Thankfully he didn't take long but, God Almighty, he let go this huge fart which echoed around the empty toilets like an opera singer in the Royal Albert Hall!

I nearly fell off the seatless lavatory that I was perched on. As soon as I heard him return to his bunk and slam the door shut to his chorus of sexual innuendoes, I tiptoed down the stairs at a very rapid rate of knots. By the time I reached the bottom and was clearing the main door I heard this almighty scream of horror, followed by a very loud yelping sound, followed by what sounded like a female lamenting. Then it was like a dawn chorus of profanities! I didn't look back but ran like fuck, once again sticking to the shadows until I got as far as the stables where I did have a quick glance over my shoulder. Satisfied that I was clear of danger, I slowed down to a stroll, began to whistle *Paddy's Day* and swaggered back to D Lines to meet up with the boys who would now be back from Guildford.

CHAPTER 4

THE FOLLOWING MORNING WE WERE ON OUR way to Thetford for, hopefully, our final exercise.

Vic Buckley, who had served with Pat a few years before, left the army and gone into civvy street for about five years, had re-joined the Micks. After successfully completing an assortment of assessments, including drill, weapon handling etc., he leapfrogged into our platoon to complete his refresher training. Being in his late twenties he had been around the houses and back again, and was without doubt the unofficial Godfather to us youngsters. Vince and 'Hovis' made sure he fitted in and didn't teach us kids too many bad habits *(I think)!*

Our platoon had passed all the endurance tests that the powers that be could possibly have thrown at us, and we made our return journey to Pirbright, absolutely triumphant!

All of us gave a fuckin' big cheer as we pulled out of the Thetford battle camp and another as we drove through the main gates of the Guards Depot. Apart from end-of-course administration and our passing out parade, it was all over bar the shouting.

There were no more embuggerance factors for our last ten days at Pirbright. We were treated as *'Almost Guardsmen'.* And it was fuckin' great!

I found out via the jungle drums that Ginge the Grenadier had been RTUd *(Returned To Unit)* for being drunk and causing several fights in and around the Guards Depot looking for some Mick called *Spud!* Thankfully I didn't run into his mate Geordie again!

The next ten days flew past. Most of our time was spent rehearsing for our passing out parade on the drill square. Apart from a well-needed visit to the barber's shop, we managed a couple of trips to the swimming pool, only on these occasions we were actually allowed to enjoy ourselves!

Then one day I got the surprise of my life. Vince McEllen told me that Mammy and Paddy had made it over from Belfast for the passing out parade and that they were staying with Pat and Pam for the duration of their visit. I was over the moon! Vince arranged for me to be made available to be collected by Pat so as I could spend a few hours one evening with Mammy and Paddy at his house, which was only a short distance from the Guard Room.

When I arrived, Mammy had to look twice to make sure it was me; after all, she hadn't seen me for about six months, and according to both her and Paddy I had really changed. I think they meant that I'd grown up PDQ *(Pretty Damn Quick)!*

Goodness me! They couldn't get a word in; I couldn't stop talking. I tried to fit in all of my training experiences in about fifteen minutes. Pat and Pam started to laugh, thus rescuing Mammy and Paddy from having to tell me to slow down and take a breath!

Pat then explained to me that, due to circumstances regarding the ongoing troubles in Belfast at that time, it had been decided by the MOD that taking leave there after the passing out parade would be frowned upon. Therefore my travel warrant had been changed to Dublin and I would stay at Robert and Anne's address for all or part of my leave period. Mammy and Paddy didn't go into too much detail, but I was to find out the full extent of the effect that the troubles had on this elderly couple at a later date.

I didn't have a problem with the decision but was a wee bit disappointed at not being able to visit Belfast. I was really looking forward to seeing the Gang of Four, among others, and boasting about my exploits at Pirbright and my imminent trip to Hong Kong. But as they say, 'C'est la vie'.

Then, the big day came. With 'Hovis' as Right Guide, Vince as Left Guide, Pat at the rear, and Tim Purdon our platoon commander in front, the final day of our training course at the Guards Depot was right there, right in front of us!

THE PASSING OUT PARADE!!!!!!!

The music was supplied by the Guards Depot Corps of Drums, who were absolutely fantastic and more than helped to enhance the grandeur that the occasion deserved.

Not a foot was put wrong, not a rifle was slack, all heads were held high and all had straight backs!

After a light lunch and even lighter refreshments, we all made a mad dash to hand over our accommodation, collect our travel warrants, and most important of all, collect our pay and extra leave money. I paid a visit to Pat and Pam's to say a quick bye-bye to Mammy and Paddy, then without further ado, John Cunningham, Tony Kerrigan and I made our way to Brookwood railway station. Our journey took us to London and then onwards to Holyhead, catching the ferry to Dun Laoghaire, and finally another, but short, train ride to Dublin.

The three of us had great craic for about a week with me using Robert and Anne's as a base. I had let the powers that be in Pirbright know that I would be spending only one week in Dublin and the remaining two in and around London. It would give me a chance to see most of the rest of the family, as well as spending time with Mammy and Paddy, before returning to Pirbright prior to heading away to Hong Kong.

All but one of the Micks turned up for duty back at Pirbright: Tony Kerrigan! I couldn't believe that anyone would complete the course at the Guards Depot and then choose not to go to somewhere like the Far East!

He certainly didn't make any mention of it when we were on leave in Dublin. John Cunningham explained to me in private that Tony and his parents couldn't get their head round being seven and a half thousand miles apart for well over a year without any sort of leave period. Tony was one of many good friends that I had made since joining the Army and I was saddened, but understood his decision not to return. I've never seen him again but would certainly love to.

With only about a week before beginning our deployment to Hong Kong, the rest of the boys and I had a few good nights out in Woking, Guildford and, of course, a Saturday night out in London. There were no restrictions on reporting back to the Guard Room for booking-in, just so long as we all got back in one piece; and not too fuckin' late!

Then one bright sunny day we were on our way to Brize Norton for an overnight stay, prior to boarding the plane for the twenty-four-hour journey to our long-awaited destination. I was lucky enough to get a window seat, and I have to say that during the daylight hours the weather was glorious, with hardly a cloud in the beautiful blue sky, and with the most beautiful and amazing scenery possibly known to man. I was gobsmacked, to say the least.

We stopped for about two hours on two occasions, once in Bahrain, and once in Singapore where we left the aircraft to stretch our legs and have a mosey around, but unfortunately we were confined to those particular airports. To be quite honest, the only downside of the whole journey was the fact that we were only allowed soft drinks or hot beverages either on the plane or in the stop-off airports; thus was the rule, and probably still is when you are travelling with the RAF! But hey, they are reputedly the safest Airline in the World!

Anyway, when the captain announced that we would soon be landing at Kai Tak Airport in Hong Kong my heart almost missed a beat; and so did everyone else's when on the same announcement he informed us that we would be approaching the runway via airspace that would be very close to the skyscrapers, but we were not to worry! Worry? Fuckin' worry! I did more than fuckin' worry. I nearly filled me fuckin' underpants! And I wasn't the only one! Some of my fellow passengers had their eyes shut tight, with their knuckles white tight around the arms of their seats!

The people in the high-rise flats were waving at us from their windows. Some of them were hanging out their fuckin' washin'! I could nearly see the whites of their fuckin' eyes!

After all these years of Hong Kong being a British colony, couldn't they have found an easier way in? It must have been some fuckin' dickhead with a degree in assholes that thought this up; and I thought it was just army officers that were supposed to be fuckin' dickheads!

Three Hail Marys and an Act of Contrition later, we landed safe and sound; well, the word 'sound' could be judged as debatable, but at least the maniac driving the fuckin' plane got us back to Planet Earth in one fuckin' piece!

As we stepped off the plane we were greeted with a very hot and sticky climate, with an unusual and slightly offensive whiff of stale air. It reminded me of the smelly sock syndrome often experienced in the Guard Room when performing overnight barrack duties! An aroma I had never experienced before during daylight hours, but I was soon to become accustomed to downtown colonial anomalies. Now, the airport was situated on the mainland of the colony known as Kowloon and the New Territories so we travelled by coach to the Wan Chai Ferry in Kowloon, then made a short but most marvellous crossing of the harbour to the island of Hong Kong – goggle-eyed all the way there – continuing our coach journey to Stanley Fort which was about a half-hour away on the south side of the island. Once again I was continuously goggle-eyed for the last leg of our journey.

When we arrived at Stanley Fort, the married families that had made the journey with us from the UK alighted from the coach just inside the main gate and were guided to their married quarters; then off the remainder of us went to one of the barrack blocks where we would be accommodated for our two weeks Draft Training. Vic Buckley was quickly processed, and posted to Support Company almost immediately due to his experience.

We were met by two L/Sgts, Bobby McMullen and Jimmy Nicholson, who were much more welcoming than the NCOs on my first day at Pirbright. I have to say it was indeed a very pleasant surprise. We were given the programme for our two-week course which, on reading, contained another very pleasant surprise. Now, Draft Training is meant to be an assessment for each new arrival, to ascertain where their natural talents could be well put to use, and also an introduction to battalion life while bringing all the top personalities to the fore. This would include drill, weapon handling, signals and basic fitness. However, all these disciplines would take place in the first week, with the second week dedicated to the rehearsals and taking part in a large Guard of Honour for an official visit by HRH Princess Anne! I developed an immediate *eee*rection!

The following morning we were introduced to the warrant officer who would be overseeing our progress throughout our draft training: none other than CSM Denis Cleary from Dublin. Denis went on to become the Regimental Sergeant-Major, then the Academy Sergeant-Major at the Royal Military Academy, Sandhurst; and if that wasn't enough, he was awarded the MBE!!!

The following days flew past with me, personally, having the time of my life and, believe it or not, enjoying every minute of it, especially when I made my frequent visits to the open-air swimming pool. 'Hovis' and Vince had certainly done more than their fair share at Pirbright to produce an extremely high level of newly trained Micks!

The big day came for Princess Anne's arrival, and as the Guard of Honour marched through downtown Hong Kong to the music of the Corps of Drums and the Pipes and Drums, I couldn't help but feel as proud as punch! The sounds of our Foot and Arms drill when we arrived at the Royal Navy HQ, *HMS Taymar*, was deafening, with the echoes of our labours resonating around the highrise buildings and skyscrapers that surrounded us:

I *eee*jaculated!

On our return to barracks, us Draftees, or Daftees as we were sometimes referred to, were instructed to pack all our kit as we would be deployed to our various companies the following afternoon. As it would be our last night together we decided to go down town for a few jars. Some of us had been out once before but didn't have sufficient funds to make a real party of it. However, on this occasion, we had just been paid. We all met in town at the China Fleet Club, close to an area known as the Wanch. With its girlie bars, discos, night clubs, massage parlours and brothels, it was sometimes referred to as *Land of a Thousand Arses!* One of the more popular catchphrases used by the local female population, young and old, was, *"Hey, Johnny! You want **Sucky Sucky**?"*

Needless to say, we all got legless, tried to sing songs, tried to play ten pin bowls, tried to sing songs, tried to do an oul dance, tried to sing songs, tried to chat up oul ones, tried to sing songs, tried to get a leg over, tried to sing songs, tried to eat a fish supper, tried to, tried to… Ah, Fuck It! Tried To Sing Songs!

The next morning I was singing to *the Big White Phone!*

Thankfully we were not required on parade until half past ten, which gave us all time to get our act together and present ourselves in an orderly manner. Joe Coyle, Jimmy Walsh and I were informed that we were being posted into Number Two Company. Now, the majority of the battalion was accommodated in barracks in Stanley Fort; however, Support Company and Number Two Company were accommodated on the west side of Hong Kong Island in a barracks known as Lei Mune. It took just under half an hour for the opentop Land Rover, with the three of us and all of our kit, to complete the journey to the block that was to be our home for the next year or so. Every so often Jimmy would have a wee kit check over the side of the vehicle with Joe following in quick succession on each occasion, with me smiling as I had puked up everything that I had consumed over the past twenty-four hours as soon as my feet had touched the floor that morning!

Me poor wee belly was well and truly empty, as were Joe's and Jimmy's, when we finally arrived at Two Company. I suspect we were pretty close to dehydration, but the odd slug from our water bottles and the gentle breeze in and around the Land Rover helped us to survive.

As we made our way through the breathtaking scenery, with high-peaked hills and narrow passes, and with not a cloud in the bright blue sky, I couldn't help but appreciate the array of different colours of the rock faces and the silent green watery fields, enhanced by the enthusiastic hand-waving of the locals. Well, they were either welcoming us or telling us to fuck off! I have to say that none of us were in any condition to care.

With my eighteenth birthday just six weeks away, followed by Christmas and New Year, there would be many more escapades in the not too distant future, that I would be able to tell the boys about back home.

For just a wee moment, I drifted away into a wee world of my own, and I thought to myself: Hey, Boy! You've come a long way.

From Belfast To Hong Kong!